JIMMY BRESLIN ON:

Congressman "Tip" O'Neill:
"He began making pencil marks on the program for the next race. 'Class really tells when there is no class,' he said. This is a saying older than the race track we were sitting in. It was direct evidence of part of the higher education O'Neill received as a youth, training that was to prove of inestimable value."

Congressman Peter Rodino:
"Rodino listened to the taped voice of Richard Nixon: 'The Italians . . . they're not like us . . . they smell different, they look different, act different . . .' Nixon's voice dropped. 'Of course the trouble is . . . the trouble is, you can't find one that's honest.' A great sadness came over Peter Rodino."

Special Counsel John Doar:
"Doar sat in a chair alongside Rodino's desk. There is in John Doar, under his silence and under his mixture of propriety and informality, a terribly fierce fifteen-round fighter. Peter Rodino, who grew up in a tenement in the First Ward of Newark, sensed this immediately."

THE CRITICS

"More books will be written about the impeachment summer, but none will be zestier or funnier. None will convey a more vivid sense."
—*The New York Times Sunday Book Review*

"THE BEST OF THE LOT . . . THE ONE MOST WORTH READING . . . BY A STREET-WISE VERBAL BRAWLER WITH A POLICE REPORTER'S EYE."
—*Time*

"Breslin's premise is this: 'Why don't we take a walk away from the convicts and step into shafts of sunlight provided by some of the people who worked for their country, rather than against it. People who are so much more satisfying to know, and to tell of. It makes a strong story—power politics, sacrifice, courage, finesse, timing, endurance. And Breslin adds enough personality profile and personal musings to straightforward reporting to recreate the atmosphere and events with emotional clarity."
—*Kansas City Star*

ON BRESLIN

"A dandy book to be read with both pleasure and edification . . . filled with jewel-like asides and juicy scoops that could only come from hard reporting."
—*Chicago Sun-Times*

"JIMMY BRESLIN JUST HAPPENS TO BE WEIGHT-FOR-AGE ONE OF THE BEST WRITERS OF OUR DAY."

—Harrison E. Salisbury
The New York Times

"Marvelously constructed, crammed with both Breslin's wit and wonderful gems of information that only a crack reporter can unearth . . . Jack Kennedy, the campaigner, pocketing a pile of cash from a fund-raising breakfast . . . Jeb Magruder still trying to be a fixer while in jail . . . Nixon making incredibly stupid ethnic slurs—and awkwardly joshing Henry Kissinger about being 'in bed with a broad' . . . Nixon's top aides' dismay upon discovering that 'the Old Man has been s----ing us.'"

—*Chicago News*

How The Good Guys Finally Won

*Notes from an
Impeachment Summer*

Jimmy Breslin

BALLANTINE BOOKS • NEW YORK

All rights reserved. Published in the United States by Ballantine Books, a division of Random House, Inc., New York, and simultaneously in Canada by Ballantine Books of Canada, Ltd., Toronto, Canada.

We wish to thank the Jerry Vogel Music Co., Inc. for permission to use lyrics from "I'll Be with You in Apple Blossom Time."

Library of Congress Catalog Card Number: 75-6706

ISBN 0-345-25001-X-175

This edition published by arrangement with The Viking Press, New York

Manufactured in the United States of America

First Ballantine Books Edition: April, 1976

for Jim Shanahan

Contents

"Guilty"

* * *

It was as graceless at the end as it was at the start.

The room was dim in the late afternoon and a heavy rain beat on the smeared windows. The room, one of the witness rooms on the second floor of the Federal Courthouse in Washington, was being used by defendants in the Watergate case as they waited for the jury to come in. William Hundley, the lawyer for John Mitchell, was standing in the doorway, taking the quick last drags on his cigarette.

"A note," he said.

"A note?" one of the other lawyers in the room said.

"A note," Hundley said.

"A verdict?"

"All I know is the jury sent in a note."

The lawyer spoke in a low voice to Hundley. "I hope we don't get a verdict today. My guy's not in shape to handle it."

"Well, you better go in there with him now," Hundley said. Hundley knew it was a verdict.

The lawyer walked out.

"Who does he have?" someone asked Hundley.

He bent down, taking the final drag on his cigarette before dropping it onto the floor.

"Mardian."

The hallway outside, empty all day, now was filled with reporters running to get places in line at the doors to the second-floor courtroom. As Hundley came out of the witness room, John Mitchell, courtroom gray stained into his face, passed by, his walk heavy. Hundley followed him. As we left the dim waiting room, the windows suddenly became filled with bright white light. Outside in the rain the television men, plastic parkas and wet beards, were turning on their equipment.

It was 4:25 p.m. of an empty New Year's Day, 1975, and now it was all coming to an end.

The windowless courtroom was too bright, the neon ceiling lights glaring off the blond-paneled walls. This type of American ceremony has no richness to it; dark tragedies are played out in flat, harsh civil-service surroundings. The five defendants already were in the courtroom when the doors were opened for reporters. There were less than a dozen ordinary spectators. At the start of the sequence of trouble, there are large crowds of the curious and knots of close friends shielding you from the curious. As the case wears on, and next week becomes next month, the curious go elsewhere and the close friends live their own lives, and at the end you always are alone with fear.

The five defendants sit at separate tables with their lawyers. Haldeman. The forehead seeming a little too large for the rest of his head. A great deal of darkness about his eyes. Ehrlichman, thin-rimmed glasses, a bulging briefcase at his feet. He carries it with him every day, the sides of the bag swelling with each new proceeding, each new document. My case. The man in the most trouble in a courtroom always carries the most papers. Mitchell, sitting up against the wall, saying something to Hundley, who tries to smile. Mardian, lips pursed, eyes glaring, frightened. Parkinson, dull, clerkish, a cipher.

It was 4:35 and they waited in the courtroom. Along the wall in the front of the room were two easels used for exhibits during the case. One of the easels had been tipped over. The large white card on it carried a heading, "White House Chart." The squares showed which man was where in the times when they all thought the power they had was real and permanent. The card on the other easel said, "Committee to Re-Elect President." Titles out of the past.

The doorknob on the door in the front of the room, to the left of the bench, rattled noisily, metallically. The courtroom froze. A loud click. The door opened. A gray-haired clerk, carrying a sheaf of papers, walked in and sat at the table in front of the bench. Who knows what the papers were? Clerks in courtrooms always carry papers. Movement came back to the people in the harsh lighted room.

The doorknob rattled again. Movement in the courtroom froze again. Another loud click. Another clerk walked in carrying another sheaf of papers.

The defendants followed the clerk as he walked to his seat.

Minutes went by. It was 4:40 now. Reporters were standing, looking at the defendants, making notes of what they were seeing, their hands shaking in the tension.

The doorknob rattled again. Silence in the room. Now the click. An immense black marshal, head shaved, looked into the room.

"All ready?" he said to the gray-haired clerk.

"All ready," the clerk said.

The marshal went out the door but did not shut it

entirely. Now, without a sound, the door swung open. The marshal slammed his hand on the wood.

"All rise," the gray-haired clerk said.

Into the harsh light came the judge, John Sirica. He went to his seat quickly, his face expressionless. He sat down and immediately turned to the marshal.

"Bring in the jury."

The marshal leaned out into the hallway behind the courtroom and stood there a moment, his hand on the door, and now there was another marshal in the hallway and behind him came the jury. They went to their seats with the shoes of the black women jurors sounding loudly on the wooden floor of the jury box. There was something pink around the neck of one of the women. There was an older woman, sparse gray wiry hair pulled straight back, hands folded in her lap. Old black woman sitting in a train station. Instead, she was passing judgment on a man who was the Attorney General of the United States. The foreman, somber, in brown, held a large brown envelope, a civil-service envelope.

The gray-haired clerk, James Capitanio, asked the foreman to rise.

"Has the jury reached a verdict?"

"Yes, they have." John A. Hoffar was the foreman.

He held out the civil-service envelope. The dark-haired clerk walked up and took it from him. The clerk took the envelope to the bench. It was 4:48. Everybody in the courtroom sat with mouths partly opened, breathing against nerves. The two clerks stood at the bench, backs to the courtroom, while Sirica opened the large envelope. He had trouble getting the papers out. He held the envelope up, reached into it, and began taking sheets of long white paper out. He put on his glasses and began reading the papers. One of the clerks shook the envelope to be certain it was empty. Sirica was saying something as he went over each paper, the clerks mumbling something back. At 4:49, Sirica still was reading and the clerks still mumbling with him. The mouths in the courtroom became a little more open. At 4:50, Sirica nodded, his head came up, and he sat back. His face showed nothing.

"The clerk will read the verdict. Defendants stand."

James Capitanio turned around, the papers in his hands. There was only this slight movement of the papers to show Capitanio had any nerves about what he was doing.

And now, around the room, the five men stood up. Their wives, tight short hair, woolen suits, sitting in the first row. The five defendants who would have ruled a nation in their way, standing so that a clerk could tell them of their future. From where I sat, only Mitchell's, Mardian's, and Parkinson's faces were visible.

Capitanio began to read in a flat courtroom voice.

"Docket number seventy-four dash one hundred ten.

"As to the defendant John N. Mitchell:

"Count one. Guilty.

"Count two. Guilty.

"Count three. Guilty.

"Count four. Guilty.

"Count five. Guilty.

"Count six. Guilty.

"Signed, John A. Hoffar, foreman."

Mitchell's face had little flecks of white paste showing in the gray. He flinched, just slightly but enough to show it to you, as the guilty-guilty-guilty hit him in the face. He looked like a man who was starting to drown but was embarrassed by it and did not want anybody to think he needed assistance.

Capitanio went without pause into the next set of papers.

"As to the defendant Harry R. Haldeman:

"Count one. Guilty.

"Count two. Guilty.

"Count seven. Guilty.

"Count eight. Guilty.

"Count nine. Guilty.

"Signed, John A. Hoffar, foreman."

The papers switched around in Capitanio's hands.

"As to the defendant John Ehrlichman:

"Count one. Guilty.

"Count two. Guilty.

"Count three. Guilty.

"Count twelve. Guilty.

"Signed, John A. Hoffar, foreman."

Only an execution carries more formal pain, and disturbs more, than this scene of men standing and listening to their lives being ruined.

"As to the defendant Robert Mardian:

"Count one. Guilty."

Mardian's head moved from right to left, as if he had just been hit with a left hook. He looked at the jury and at the door and at the wall and at the people in the first rows. He looked for something, for somebody, to tell him that it never had been said, that this clerk in the front of the room had not said he was guilty. Face flushed, mouth open, eyes darting, Mardian looked for help.

Robert Mardian had stood on the balcony of the Justice Department in the gloom of the late afternoon in the fall of 1969, stood there behind John Mitchell and Richard Kleindienst. Sometimes Mardian was off the balcony and inside the office. But you always could see his face. Out on the balcony, inside the office, when the curtains parted. His face was red with anger and his mouth was contorted. He was pointing, the finger jabbing the air in anger, at the young people who were running through the tear gas in the street below. A huge antiwar demonstration had just ended at the Washington Monument. A couple of thousand, students mostly, many of them high-school students, had marched to the Justice Department. Some of them were looking for what they felt was trouble: climbing, window-breaking, raising a Viet Cong flag on the empty flagpole. They were the older ones, lost in the ridiculous dream of being Weathermen. Aside from these few—police could have easily handled them— the crowd was made up of students. And Mardian stood snarling and shaking with anger, and standing in front of him, Mitchell smoked a pipe. Kleindienst watched to see that his orders had been carried out— that the students were met with tear gas and United States Marshals. And here on the street in front of the Justice Department was a young girl, fourteen, laugh- ing and skipping through the patches of tear gas. On the balcony, Robert Mardian's face became the deepest red. In front of Mardian, John Mitchell sourly sucked on his pipe. Later, over Scotch, he would say that they all should be arrested and deported to Rus- sia. Next to Mitchell on the balcony was Richard Kleindienst, then the assistant Attorney General. Agents were tapped on the shoulder, orders were given to use more tear gas, to make more arrests, to go to the wooden clubs against these Communist hordes, these fourteen-year-old girls running through the tear gas. It was, on that late fall afternoon, a scene from another country—with the mean and powerful men standing on a balcony. And another country is pre- cisely what John Mitchell's Justice Department at- tempted to make out of the United States.

And now, here in court, on New Year's Day, John Mitchell stood convicted of enormous crimes against the old America, the America that has a Constitution. And Richard Kleindienst already had pleaded guilty and had squirmed and cried his way out of a prison sentence. He went home hoping to be regarded as a man who was misunderstood. And Robert Mardian was looking wildly around a courtroom for help that was not to come.

Parkinson's verdict was read next. He was not guilty, the clerk said. Parkinson's lawyers slapped him on the back. John Mitchell looked across the room to him, his mouth forming the word, "Congratulations." Only

Mitchell did this. The others stood in their own trouble. The defendants were told to sit down. Mardian sat heavily. His face came into his hands.

The jury was sent home after a couple of words from Sirica. James Neal, the prosecutor, slipped up to the bench. He told Sirica that he was leaving the job as of that moment. Neal had come up from Nashville to do what he had to do. He had disliked doing it. Neal does not prosecute for pleasure. Sirica said, "Thank you for your service to the country." Neal went back to his seat and stared at the table. He wanted what was coming next to be over as quickly as possible. He wanted to get out of the room, out of the building, out of Washington.

Sirica looked at the papers in front of him. He moved them away from him. He picked up something else, looked at it. Then his head came up.

"Now . . ."

With the one word—"Now . . ."—it was all different. No longer was it a matter of guilt, of proving who was responsible for Watergate, for the attempted theft of something of national value. "Now" meant that this phase was over. And it had become time for the arrangements for punishment to be made, for dates to be set with probation officers, for pre-sentencing reports, for consideration of placing men into prisons.

Everything became dark. Once is too many times to be around things like this. The moment I could, I strayed out of the courtroom. Mardian was in his chair, motionless. His wife came up to place a hand on his elbow. Mardian brushed her off. In the prizefighting business they used to call a guy like this a mutt.

I went back into an office they were using as a press-room to pick up my raincoat. Ehrlichman came in with his wife. Reporters clustered around him and he answered questions, his finger jabbing out somebody whose hand was up. The finger motion was accompanied with a little compression of the lips. The

German love for the mannerisms of authority is per-
vasive. I asked him if he didn't think it was time for
Richard Nixon to come out of his house and take a
little bit of the weight, assume the responsibility, in
this matter that was wrecking so many lives. Ehrlichman listened to that question, looked up for a moment,
nodded his head—Now I know what you mean—and
began his answer. "I respect your opinion, but I just
answered that question in words within the judicial
framework. Ah . . ." He started down a trail which I
did not understand. He was speaking in off-English, in
words which seemed one half notch off true meaning.
He spoke earnestly, affably, but with one foot out of
bounds. In the White House one day, Ehrlichman had
proclaimed that all government investigatory resources
should converge upon Larry O'Brien so that O'Brien
would be put into a prison before the 1972 election.
Yet standing in the pressroom, trying to talk, getting
a subordinate meaning out of anything said to him,
Ehrlichman was a mournful figure. Why is it that the
science of getting even always becomes desolate at the
end?

Nixon's presence would have made things far
gloomier. Apparently, Nixon was perfectly capable of
being the worst defendant ever. Early in the going,
Nixon is supposed to have mentioned something about
committing suicide. And Haig supposedly said, "That
might be an idea worth considering." And Nixon
didn't speak to Haig for about a week.

I left as Ehrlichman droned on. Outside the building, H. R. Haldeman was standing in the rain in front
of the television cameras. There was nothing profitable
in listening to him. In the end, all convicted criminals
are boring.

Back at the Jefferson Hotel, the bar and restaurant
were closed for the holiday weekend. The only sound
in the lobby was the desk clerk turning the pages of
a newspaper. I went upstairs to pack. I left the door
to my room open. From a suite down the hall I could

hear a loud voice, a hysterical voice, and the sounds of other voices trying to calm everything down. Mardian in John Mitchell's suite. It was to take Mitchell two hours to get Mardian in some form of control of himself.

The voices were quite loud, drumming in the ears, while I waited for the elevator. It was a relief to step on the elevator, and have the doors close against the sound. I don't want to hear them, or hear much about them again. For there were too many decent people, people with honesty and dignity and charm, who were an important part of the summer of 1974 in Washington, the summer in which the nation forced a President to resign from office. And if we are going to talk about the end of Watergate, as we are about to do here, why don't we take a walk away from the convicts and step into the shafts of sunlight provided by some of the people who worked for their country, rather than against it. People who are so much more satisfying to know, and to tell of.

1

"...impeachment is going to hit this Congress."

* * *

He doesn't remember the date, he wasn't keeping notes on everything at the time, but Congressman Thomas P. O'Neill, Jr., does know that it was just after he had become Majority Leader of the House of Representatives in January of 1973 that he walked into Speaker Carl Albert's office and said, "All my years tell me what's happening. They did so many bad things during that campaign that there is no way to keep it from coming out. They did too many things. Too many people know about it. There is no way to keep it quiet. The time is going to come when impeachment is going to hit this Congress and we better be ready for it."

His opinion was not received with great warmth. The House of Representatives is not a place of positive action. It is an institution designed only to react, not to plan or lead. O'Neill had not often broken the rule. Albert's caution begins with breakfast. To speak of impeaching Richard Nixon was like asking him to use his shoetip to inspect for landmines. As O'Neill persisted in his conversation, Peter W. Rodino, Jr., was asked to the meeting. Through his years in Congress, Rodino had shown great natural cautiousness; he once took the grave risk of getting out front to pass a bill declaring Columbus Day a national holiday. And at this time, early in 1973, Rodino had just been made Chairman of the House Judiciary Committee, and thus was moving even more hesitantly than usual.

* * *

When you see Peter Rodino now, today, he sits in the back of a car, the windows open to the chill of a fall evening, and somebody in the car tries to close the window but there are so many people on the sidewalk pushing their hands and faces into the car to say hello to Peter Rodino that the window cannot be closed. The people are at the bus stop on Roosevelt Avenue, in the Flushing section of Queens, in New York City, and one of them, a woman, puts her head into the car and says she is Rae Grossman. "For what you did for America," she says, "can I go get you a cup of coffee?" "Thank you," Peter Rodino says, "but we're leaving in just a moment now." "For what you did for this country just let me get a cup of coffee for you," she says. "No, thank you very much, but we're leaving," Rodino says. Outside the car, in the wind swirling up the block, the people coming home from work take a quick look at Rodino and then, talking excitedly, jam onto buses.

* * *

However, when it started, when Rodino was a Congressman from Newark whom nobody knew, Rodino regarded impeachment as a word that had danger hanging from it the instant it left the mouth. Rodino pointed out to O'Neill that there was absolutely nothing to go on. This irritated O'Neill. Of course he had something to go on. What was it? Why, he had what he just said, that an impeachment was going to hit this Congress and they all had better be ready for it.

* * *

There was one Sunday, in the summer of 1974, when O'Neill was talking about how it all started. O'Neill was at Harwichport, on Cape Cod, and the church traffic had the main street in town tied up. I got to O'Neill's long ranch house at 12:15, just as O'Neill was going out of the house into the early summer heat. The lawn was wet and trees were dripping. He got into a well-used Impala, put a pack of Daniel Webster cigars on the dashboard for the trip, and then we started driving to Boston, two hours away.

"I'll tell you how it happened, but of course you can't use any of this," he began. In the weeks to come, I would learn that he began practically every conversation with everybody in this manner, and those who heeded him, who did not write what he was saying, almost invariably woke up in the morning to find it printed in some other place.

"Now," O'Neill went on, "I was the Chairman of the Democratic Congressional campaign dinner in Washington, and because of that I got to know every big giver to the Democratic party in the nation. We had a guy everywhere to organize and to get you the money. You take New York, we got a dozen in New York. Jim Wilmot, Mary Lasker, Abe Feinberg, Gene Wyman did a terrific job for the party in California. And when he died his wife kept going for us. My job was to come in at the end and talk to them, and then to talk to anybody they had been contacting. I did the asking. Substantial contributors, I knew the majority of them in the country. You need them. There's no way it can be done without them until the entire system changes. As it is now, there are four parts to any campaign. The candidate, the issues of the candidate, the campaign organization, and the money to run the campaign with. Without the money you can forget the other three.

"Well, I can tell you that I started hearing from a lot of them. There would be a guy who always was a big giver and nobody was hearing from him. I'd go over the lists for our dinner and I'd say, 'Hey, where is so and so? He always was a helluva good friend of ours. Why haven't we heard from him?' So I'd call the guy and he'd call me back and he'd say, 'Geez, Tip, I don't know what to tell you. Nine IRS guys hit me last week and I'd like to stay out of things for a while.' I began getting that from a lot of people. Fellows like George Steinbrenner. He's a helluva guy. I called him up and I said, 'George, old pal, what's the matter? Why don't we hear from you any more? Is something the matter?' You bet I called him up. He was one of these guys who would get on the phone for you and raise up a half dozen other guys to come and help out. So what does Steinbrenner say to me? He said, 'Geez, Tip, I want to come to see you and tell you what's going on.' And he came into my office. He said, 'Gee, they are holding the lumber over my head.' They got him between the IRS, the Justice Department, the Commerce Department. He was afraid he'd lose his business.

"Believe me, when they start doing IRS audits on you, there is no way that they're not going to get something on you if they want to. No way. So I talked it over with Steinbrenner and what do you think he told me they wanted off him? He said Stans's people wanted a hundred thousand dollars for Nixon's campaign. And then they wanted him to be the head of Democrats for Nixon in Ohio. He told me he'd been in to see them and this is what they told him. Well, there was nothing we could do to help him at that

point. These other guys had taken
can party. They had set up inde
That would cripple the Republica
they were going to cripple the Dem
George to do what he had to do. Geor̶
think he was going to give in. Then he left the ̶
and I don't know what he did. He went over to see
this Kalmbach or somebody like that. I guess he had
no choice. This Maurice Stans. He has to be the lousi-
est bastard ever to live. Now, I was getting this from
all over. Guys began to come in and see me and say,
'Tip, I'm having trouble with a contract. I never had
trouble before. It's legitimate business. They tell me to
see Stans. What can I do?'

"That's what it was like. All our old friends, our
best friends, were afraid to come around. Well, you
didn't have to draw a map for me to let me know what
was going on. It was a shakedown. A plain old-
fashioned goddammed shakedown. I can read pressure. I could see what they were doing. And then out
comes this great big newspaper ad. Democrats for
Nixon. And the ad had all the names of our people on
it. The day the ad came out, they were calling me up
saying, 'Tip, I had to sign the ad. They sandbagged
me. It's either sign the ad or go into the soup.' Well, I
kept saying to myself, this Nixon and Stans have got
to be kidding. What they're doing is too big. You
never can get away with a thing like this. Not in this
country. But they were sure trying. Now I don't remember when I said it, but I know I said to myself
somewhere in the 1972 campaign. I said, 'This fellow
is going to get himself impeached.' The strange thing
about it is that I never gave much thought to the Watergate break-in when it happened. I thought it was
silly and stupid. I never thought it was important. I
was concentrating on the shakedown of these fellas
like Steinbrenner."

This ride ended in the rain in the parking lot of Suffolk Downs Race Track in East Boston. The occasion

he thirty-ninth running of the Massachusetts
dicap. They ran the 1974 Race on a Sunday and
homas (Tip) O'Neill was going to be there no matter
what. In his life, only a swearing-in is more important
than Mass Handicap Day. Inside the track, on his way
to the dining room, O'Neill shook hands with a head-
waiter, with Joe Dugan, an old New York Yankee third baseman, and with Rip Valente, the fight
promoter. O'Neill sat at a window table and looked
over the menu. "I'm going to eat something very
light," he said. He put the menu down. "A New England boiled dinner and a bottle of beer," he told the
waiter. When the food came, he looked at the scattered strips of corned beef on his plate. "Bring us a
whole plate of corned beef on the side," he said. He
put his glasses on and began making pencil marks on
the program for the next race. "Class really stands out
when there is no class," he said. This is a race-track
saying older than the race track we were sitting in. It
was direct evidence of part of the higher education
O'Neill received as a youth, training of inestimable
value to a person who, someday, was going to push for
impeachment of a President. For at the race track,
where life is uncoated and speech is direct, there is an
extraordinarily keen awareness of the possibilities of
larceny jumping up at any moment, in any form. And
a man who spent time at the paddock of a race track,
as Tip O'Neill did, had no trouble at all in understanding exactly what was happening to people in
this country like George Steinbrenner.

* * *

Early in 1968, at the big Democratic campaign fund-
raising dinner in Washington, great anticipation ran
through the room upon the appearance of George M.
Steinbrenner III, the owner of a shipbuilding company
in Cleveland, who was taking his first step into heavy-
weight politics. Steinbrenner was new money, which in

politics is stronger than new love. Therefore, Steinbrenner had been given a great table, right down
front, where he could be thoroughly exposed to at-
tacks by the great names of Democratic politics. A
tree facing a forest fire. But also a tree ready to join
the fire: Steinbrenner owned a company which did
business with the government.

On other counts, too, he was a natural to come into
the game. He'd been active in Cleveland, saving the
National Air Show for the city, walking through
Hough at the time of the riot in 1968, and he also was
interested in show business and sports, two distant
cousins of politics. At the end of the 1968 campaign,
Steinbrenner discovered how much of a natural for
politics he really was. Nixon had just won the election
and the Democrats were in debt $8.5 million nation-
ally and there was no money left in the Democratic
Senate and House campaign funds. At this point, Senators Daniel Inouye and Gaylord Nelson spoke to
Steinbrenner, asking him to be the chairman of the
1969 fund-raising dinner. Steinbrenner accepted. In
1969, the dinner raised $800,000 for Congressional
campaigns. The next year it brought in over a million.
Great national heroes are as prominent as waiters
when matched against a man who can raise big money
for politicians.

The record also shows that from 1968 on, Steinbrenner was in continual difficulty with the government. How much of the trouble was for legitimate
reasons—and how much of it was illegitimate (the
Nixon re-election people at work)—is impossible to
tell. Steinbrenner, over a gin at Shea Stadium in New
York—he owns the Yankees—refers you to lawyers.
The Nixon people, all either in prison or awaiting
trial, also refer you to lawyers. It is understood, however, that this was an Internal Revenue Service audit
of Steinbrenner and his businesses after 1968. So, as
O'Neill said later, there is no such thing as an audit being done and nothing being found. If the IRS auditor

doesn't find something amiss, his pencils are taken away from him and he has to write all reports with a buffalo nickel. Steinbrenner also had problems with the Commerce Department. In purchasing the American Shipbuilding Company in 1968, Steinbrenner inherited an obligation to build an oceanography research ship for the government. The ship was to cost, Steinbrenner claimed, $8 million more than originally estimated by the owners of American Shipbuilding. Each department Steinbrenner went to, Commerce and then Defense, gave him either no action or no hope. After phone calls and letters, Steinbrenner finally was given word that Maurice Stans, then Secretary of Commerce, would see that there was a hearing. In November of 1971, a Department of Defense auditing team moved into the shipbuilding company. When the audits were finished, Stans sent word that the results appeared favorable. In February of 1971, Stans ruled against Steinbrenner. In 1972 he left the Commerce Department for the job of Chairman of the Finance Committee to Re-Elect the President.

On another front, Steinbrenner also was in difficulty with the Justice Department's antitrust division. Steinbrenner had entered into negotiations to purchase the shipbuilding division of Litton Industries. The Justice Department said the purchase would be in violation of antitrust laws. Steinbrenner became involved in the purchase of a tug company, Great Lakes Towing. Again, the Justice Department said it would be in violation. All during this period, industries of any size were being allowed and encouraged to use machetes on all rules and consumers. The only anger Richard Nixon ever showed was at the least hint of a government agency preventing an industry from gouging the people of the nation. Yet all Steinbrenner, the Democratic Dinner Chairman, had was trouble. He began to entertain the notion that somebody was trying to tell him something.

Steinbrenner had in 1968 placed some of his law

business with a college classmate, Tom Evans, an attorney in the firm of Mudge, Rose, Guthrie & Alexander—formerly Nixon, Mudge, Rose, Guthrie, Alexander & Mitchell. The law firm had offices at 20 Broad Street in Manhattan. Upon senior partner Nixon's election, branch offices immediately were opened in Washington, on Pennsylvania Avenue. This did not appear to be a move to discourage potential clients who had legal problems with government agencies. If you stumbled coming out of the Mudge, Rose Washington building, you wound up banging your head into the guard booth on the White House driveway. Evans does not seem to have been of any spectacular help to Steinbrenner at first. Somewhere in their relationship, Steinbrenner asked about a possible ambassadorship for his brother-in-law Jacob Kamm, a professor at Case-Western Reserve University. The price list Steinbrenner saw for ambassadorships was too high for him, brilliant brother-in-law or not. At the start of 1972, attorney Evans and client Steinbrenner began to discuss Evans' great desire to see Richard Nixon re-elected. Steinbrenner admitted he was not in love with the thought of supporting George McGovern, who at the time was methodically putting together the Democratic nomination. At the same time, Steinbrenner primarily was in love with the thought of getting out of his problems with government agencies. Nowhere has it ever been said that American business or politics is an amateur sport. During these conversations, attorney Evans told his client, "I'm setting up a meeting for you with Herb Kalmbach."

Steinbrenner asked who Herb Kalmbach was. Evans told him that Kalmbach was the man in charge of big donors to the Nixon campaign.

Steinbrenner saw Kalmbach in the offices of the Committee to Re-Elect the President. These offices were located in the same building on Pennsylvania Avenue as the Mudge, Rose law firm. One of the beauty parts of royalty is that you don't have to be subtle. At first Steinbrenner and Kalmbach talked good, pleasant Republican talk. Football. Steinbrenner once was an assistant coach at Purdue. Kalmbach knew the names of Southern California football players.

Kalmbach then said, "I understand from Tom Evans that you're interested in contributing to the campaign."

"Yes I am," Steinbrenner said.

"Well, if you're thinking of coming in here for under a hundred thousand dollars, don't bother," Kalmbach said. "We work up to a million around here."

"That's too steep for me," Steinbrenner said.

Kalmbach preferred not to hear. At this stage, Steinbrenner was in the exact position of a person who has lost on gambling to a bookmaker, and the bookmaker, seeking to get paid, has brought the gambler to a shylock with whom the bookmaker has an alliance.

"Do you intend to do this by check or by cash?" Kalmbach said.

"By check," Steinbrenner said.

Kalmbach took two sheets from his desk. Printed on them were the various committees formed to receive contributions to the campaign. Kalmbach said, "Now, here is what I would expect of you."

In the left hand corner of the top page, Kalmbach wrote in black pen:

$$33 @ 3$$
$$1 @ 1$$

He pushed the paper across to Steinbrenner. The numbers needed no explanation: give $3000 to each of thirty-three committees on the sheets and give $1000 to one other committee. Steinbrenner could choose his committees. There were sixty listed on the sheets: Effective Government Committee, Dedicated

Americans for Government Reform, Loyal Americans for a Better America, Stable Society Committee, United Friends of Reform in Society, Reform in Society Support Group. No matter which of the exotically named committees Steinbrenner preferred, the number would come out the same: thirty-three at three and one at one equals $100,000.

"You do a lot of business in Washington, you'd do well to get with the right people," Kalmbach told Steinbrenner. In other places, other men, better men than Kalmbach, tell you, "Pay or Die."

Kalmbach has admitted to Watergate investigators, Dave Dorsen for one, that, yes, he did have this way of speaking to potential contributors and he certainly could have spoken this way to Steinbrenner. As Kalmbach sees it, all he was doing was suggesting amounts and then sort of selling, prodding perhaps, the man into making the contribution. In a district attorney's office, this method he used is known as extortion.

When Steinbrenner left Kalmbach's office, he felt he was in trouble. He knew he had gone too far with Kalmbach, and now he was afraid to say no. And with the other side contacting him, with a Tip O'Neill calling him up, he decided he had, through design and accident, put himself into a great deal of trouble. While he was in Washington, Steinbrenner spoke to Tip O'Neill, Daniel Inouye, and Edward Kennedy. He told them of Kalmbach's demands. All of them said there was nothing that could be done at the time. Everybody was helpless. Steinbrenner went home to Cleveland. Where, immediately, the phone calls began from Herbert Kalmbach. If Steinbrenner was going to contribute, Kalmbach said, he was to be certain to do so before April 7. All campaign contributions were allowed to be in secrecy before that date. Steinbrenner had his treasurer, Bob Bartolme, make out the checks for Kalmbach. Seventy-five thousand dollars of it, Steinbrenner says, came from him person-

ally. The other $25,000 was put together in the form
of bonuses to executives, the bonuses immediately
turned over to the Nixon Committee as personal do-
nations. This was breaking all laws against corporate contributions. When the checks were in order,
Bartolme sent a messenger to Washington with the
$100,000 for the re-election of Richard Nixon.

That month, in April of 1972, Steinbrenner told the
people around him that he finally was all right, that
the lawyer Evans had told him that the three people
running Washington were H. R. Haldeman, John D.
Ehrlichman, and Fred Malek, and that he, Steinbrenner, was all right with all three of them. A lawyer from
John Connally's Democrats for Nixon called Steinbrenner and asked if he would be head of Democrats
for Nixon in Ohio. Steinbrenner resisted this. He did
not make his new friends particularly happy with his
resistance, but Steinbrenner felt he had done enough.
He had. He was going to wind up with so many federal indictments against him that in August 1974 he
pleaded guilty to a felony.

* * *

For at the start of 1973, instead of having such a
smashing year with the Kalmbachs blocking for him,
Steinbrenner wound up being tackled by James Polk
of *The Washington Star-News*. Polk is first class. He
spoke to Steinbrenner about the campaign contributions made by American Shipbuilding employees.
Steinbrenner told Polk a story which Polk did not
believe. Polk then went to American Shipbuilding employees. He found an accountant who earned $16,000
in salary had contributed $3000 to Dedicated Amer-
icans for Good Government and another $3000 to
Dedicated Volunteers for a Better America. The accountant said they were personal contributions, not
corporate contributions which of course were illegal.
Polk learned that the employee had made out the cam-

paign checks at the same time he had received a surprise bonus of $6000 from American Shipbuilding. Oh, no, the employee said. His contributions had been out of patriotism. Polk printed the stories. He also called the situation to the attention of the Watergate Special Prosecutor's office at the time it was established. The Special Prosecutor's office sent FBI agents out to interview Steinbrenner and his employees.

"Don't worry about it," John H. Melcher, Jr., American Shipbuilding counsel, told the employees. He, Steinbrenner, and the employees told the same story to the FBI that they had told to Polk. Subpoenas then were issued to the employees, calling them before a grand jury. "Don't worry," Melcher told them again. This time they did worry. "He would be saying 'don't worry' to me the day I got put behind bars for perjury," one of them said.

Out of their testimony came a sixteen-count indictment against Steinbrenner and Melcher. At this point, Steinbrenner drove into the offices of Edward Bennett Williams, Attorney at Law, Washington, D.C. Any criminal lawyer I've ever spoken to has told me that if he ever got into trouble he would try to retain Williams. Life became less complicated for Steinbrenner when Williams stopped his covering up and storytelling. With Williams plea bargaining, the sixteen counts were reduced to two: illegal campaign contributions and aiding and abetting obstructions of justice.

Finally, in October of 1974, Steinbrenner entered a guilty plea in federal court in Cleveland.

Nothing ever happened on his claim of cost overruns on the oceanography research vessel. Steinbrenner has taken the case to the United States Court of Claims. He also was forced to suspend his activities as principal owner of the New York Yankee baseball team. Edward Bennett Williams asked Baseball Commissioner Bowie Kuhn, "Well, how do you explain baseball taking no action against Cesar Cedeno?" Cedeno plays centerfield for the Houston Astros, and in 1973 he was convicted in Santo Domingo of involuntary manslaughter when a gun went off in a motel room and shot a girl in the head. Kuhn said, oh, there was a difference. "After all, Cedeno did that in the off-season."

Nobody knows how many cases of this sort there were. Businessmen who were robbed would prefer to forget about it. The IRS agents burned files. They must have had a lot of burning to do, because the operation came from the top and almost nothing was considered too small. This can be attested to personally.

In the fall of 1971, a friend, Charles U. Daly, soon to be a vice president at Harvard University, had an enormously practical idea which involved Congressman Paul McCloskey, with whom Daly had served in Korea. Daly wanted to help McCloskey, a Republican, to run against Richard Nixon in the New Hampshire primary, in February, in order to bring some sort of pressure, if possible, on Nixon to stop bombing people in Vietnam. Daly and McCloskey agreed first to go to Laos and Vietnam, observe the bombing of unarmed people, then begin campaigning on that issue in New Hampshire. In order to raise funds for the trip to Asia and the start of the campaign, Daly and McCloskey came to New York, and writer Jimmy Breslin took them around for an evening of fund raising. We met in the Sherry-Netherland Hotel, which serves drinks strong enough to make a mule walk backward. We then went out into the night after money. At the third stop, an East Side cocktail party, I cornered Martin Fife, a plastics manufacturer. Fife called a gray-haired man over and introduced him as Sam Rubin, an investor. Each said he would give $1000. I told Fife and Rubin that this was a great undertaking. "The public will listen more to a McCloskey, he's a Republican who fought in a war. This isn't some freaking New York peacenik going over there, like one of these trips this Cora Weiss takes."

I walked away feeling great and reaching for another drink. How was I to know that Cora Weiss was Sam Rubin's daughter? The last stop of the night was at some high-class brownstone on the East Side. I came out of the house holding a full glass of Scotch and water, a fine crystal glass. I tripped as I hit the sidewalk. I held the precious glass up high as I went down, landing on my shoulder. The glass was safe. The butler came racing from the town-house doorway. He bent over me, snatched the fine crystal glass from my hand, then raced back inside the house. I was lying in the cold on the sidewalk and I heard the bolt clicking as the butler inside the house locked the door.

Sometime later there was a prominent newspaper story which mentioned that James Breslin, the writer, had helped raise money for the McCloskey venture. Days after the article appeared, the IRS announced in the mail that it had discovered I owed $7500 in back taxes. This was or was not a coincidence. I paid, McCloskey tried and failed to make an appreciable dent in New Hampshire, and that was the end of it.

And then in the middle of 1973, during the Ervin committee hearings, a committee staff worker handed McCloskey three sheets of paper, Xerox copies of evidence being compiled by the staff. McCloskey showed them to me. The first said:

FOR: *Attorney General*
FROM: *John Dean*

Attached is some additional information which Jack has collected re: McCloskey operation. I've passed a copy along to Jeb Magruder.

bcc Gordon Strachan

The second Xerox was of a White House Inter-Office memorandum form:

TO: *John Dean*
FROM: *John J. Caulfield*

Under the space for "Remarks" it read, "AG should see these. They are very consistent with my report."

Attached to the memo were a group of clippings, including *The New York Times* article about the McCloskey operation.

The third Xerox copy read:

TO: *John Dean, John Mitchell*
FROM: *John J. Caulfield*

On the East Coast, McCloskey has sought and has accepted what is described as "New York Peace Money." At a New York City party McCloskey raised $11,000 which was used to finance a trip to Southeast Asia. Some attending party were: Stewart Mott, left-wing philanthropist; Howard Steen, Dreyfus Fund; Sam Rubin, investor.

It was learned that writer Jimmy Breslin and former Kennedy staffer Charles Daly were instrumental in this particular effort. Daly accompanied McCloskey on the trip.

They were playing, therefore, a game that was extensive as it was dangerous. The fact that a Tip O'Neill could be aroused shows that. The man knows better than anyone else that this nation has yet to hold its first canonization of somebody who remained in a State of Grace while campaign fund raising. During the 1960 Presidential campaign, O'Neill was an advance man in Missouri for John F. Kennedy and in the course of his duties he came upon August Busch, who offered to round up thirty people for a $1000-a-head breakfast meeting if Kennedy would show up. O'Neill called Kennedy, who quickly asked the crucial question about the proposed meeting. "What time should I be there?" The breakfast was arranged at an airport motel and Kennedy arrived, stepped into the room, received the money nod from O'Neill, and then said to the guests, "If you'll excuse Congressman O'Neill and me for a moment."

The two of them went out and jammed into what O'Neill remembers as the world's smallest men's room.

"Now I have twelve thousand in cash and seventeen thousand in checks, what do you want me to do with it?" O'Neill said.

"Give the checks to Kenny O'Donnell. I'll take the cash."

O'Neill handed Kennedy the cash and watched it disappear into the inside jacket pocket.

"Geez, this business is no different if you're running for ward leader or President of the United States," O'Neill said to Kennedy.

Kennedy said nothing and the two of them went back to the breakfast.

2

"The reputation of power is power."

* * *

After the first meeting in which O'Neill remembers the word impeachment being used, the three of them, Albert, Rodino, and O'Neill went back to their business with nothing agreed upon. A few weeks later, Rodino mentioned the matter to the chief counsel of the House Judiciary Committee, Jerome Zeifman. Zeifman is the only person I ever have met who spent fifteen years in government and wound up a radical. The moment he heard impeachment the blood rose to his mouth. Zeifman already had a file on impeachment precedents put together. He had been forced to do research when the House Minority Leader, Gerald R. Ford of Michigan, acting as he always did even upon the whim of Richard Nixon, had called for impeachment of Supreme Court Justice William O. Douglas. Zeifman gathered background and precedents for impeachment and on the vague chance that the question would reach the Judiciary Committee. Which it did not. The files, however, remained, and now Zeifman could not wait to put his files to work against Richard Nixon. Somewhere in Washington there was a squealing, grinding sound, The hugest wheel in the country, bureaucracy, was starting to turn.

* * *

The problem was that there wasn't even a shred of documentation, only a race-track suspicion by one Congressman. Also the Chairman of the Judiciary Committee, Peter Rodino, had been raised by an immigrant father who taught him to hold the Presidency in respect second only to a statue in church. As Peter Rodino's father told him of the President of the United States, blue smoke appeared high in the sky over Newark and young Rodino saw enormous things appear in it. From the start of our history, most of this country lived in this manner. The Office of President is such a bastardized thing, half royalty and half democracy, that nobody knows whether to genuflect or spit. At the start, George Washington wanted to go to his first inauguration in a gilded carriage drawn by twelve white horses and insisted upon being called "His Excellency." Thomas Jefferson caused him to settle for less horsepower and less title—"Mr. President." Which accomplished nothing because now, two hundred years later, in the Rayburn Office Building, Washington, D.C., Peter Rodino was frozen by the illusion his father had created for him.

Impeachment, Jerome Zeifman said to himself. Impeachment, impeachment, impeachment. Jerome Zeifman knew John W. Dean III from the period when Dean was an assistant minority counsel on the Judiciary Committee. Zeifman knew Dean as a person who took no chances on his own; at all times John Dean wanted the full authority of everybody over him. If Dean was performing any questionable acts, then

Zeifman knew automatically that Nixon knew of all of them. And of course Dean had to be doing something wrong. Had to. Impeachment, impeachment. It came to Zeifman what he could do. He called Gary Hymel, legislative assistant in the Majority Leader's office. Hymel came around to the Judiciary Committee's offices. Zeifman worked in a space that was not enclosed. He looked around, told Hymel they could not talk in such surroundings. He led Hymel to a vacant room and locked the door.

Zeifman is short, with thinning sandy-gray hair and a slow, measured way of speaking. He will begin a sentence with a word and then stop completely as if what he is going to say next will cause a corner of the world to come to an end. He comes from East Third Street in Manhattan. Gary Hymel is tall, dark-haired, with the face of a boy who is just changing into a man. He does not look like his experience, which is long. Hymel is from New Orleans, and his predominant talent, a great one, is that of listening.

"Gary, I am convinced . . ." Zeifman paused and looked intensely at Hymel, ". . . by everything I see that there is going to be an impeachment."

"I better tell Tip about it right now," Hymel said.

He left the room and went on the subway from the Rayburn Building to the Capitol. He walked into the Majority Leader's offices and found O'Neill. He shut the door so nobody would disturb them. Then he told O'Neill of what Jerome Zeifman, chief counsel, House Judiciary Committee, had told him. *Impeachment.*

"I knew it," Tip O'Neill said.

Dammit, now we better hurry up; the thing is starting without me. I better get right onto it. Impeachment. You bet he's going to be impeached. Why, they must have it in their heads to get going right now.
.As he sat in his office, Thomas P. O'Neill, who is called Tip by most people and Tom by those who

know him well, never noticed that he had his hand
on a huge mirror that did not exist but did exist.

* * *

Tip O'Neill at all times has one great political weapon
at his disposal. He understands so well that all political power is primarily an illusion. If people think you
have power, then you have power. If people think you
have no power, then you have no power. This is a
great truth in politics that I was able to recognize in
O'Neill's ways, because I had taken the enormous
trouble to go out and learn this in the streets and
clubhouses of the City of New York and particularly
as a candidate for citywide office in 1969, an adven-
ture which left me with the deep-lasting scars of one
who went and learned the hard way, thus learning
forever. For those who take their politics from a book,
an easier but much less effective way of learning than
mine, this same proposition has been advanced in
print by Thomas Hobbes, who wrote in England in the
1600s: "The reputation of power is power." Power is
an illusion.

Illusion. Mirrors and blue smoke, beautiful blue
smoke rolling over the surface of highly polished mirrors, first a thin veil of blue smoke, then a thick cloud
that suddenly dissolves into wisps of blue smoke, the
mirrors catching it all, bouncing it back and forth. If
somebody tells you how to look, there can be seen in
the smoke great, magnificent shapes, castles and king-
doms, and maybe they can be yours. All this becomes
particularly dynamic when the person telling you
where to look knows how to adjust the mirrors, tilt
one forward, walk to the other side, and turn one on
its base a few degrees to the right, suddenly causing
the refractions to be different everywhere. And then
going to the blue smoke, lessening it, intensifying it,
and all the time keeping those watching transfixed,
hoping, believing himself. Believing perhaps more

than anybody else in the room. And at the same time knowing that what he is believing in is mirrors and blue smoke.

This is the game called politics and power as it is played in the Legion Halls and Elks Clubs and church basements and political clubhouses throughout the country, throughout the world, while men try to please and calm others in order to maintain and improve a public career. Always, no matter what country you are in, the culmination of politics is considered to be the men who are in Washington and who are the best in the world at taking an illusion and telling you, and telling themselves, that it really is power.

This thesis, this truth, never was clearer than it was in Washington in the summer of 1974. Thomas P. O'Neill, Jr., had power, great power at times, because nearly everybody in Washington thought of him as having power. In the book, *Rules and Practices of the House of Representatives,* mention is made of every rule and roost in the House. There happens not to be one single mention, direct or indirect, of a position known as Majority Leader. By law, there is no such post. There is custom for it. There also is a line in the appropriations to pay for staff salaries for the Majority Leader. The holder of the job has large offices and is driven in great limousines. But by law or custom, there is no exact definition of the duties of the Majority Leader.

When Tip O'Neill decided that his primary duty was to make rapid the removal of Richard Nixon he took on great power. Because everybody began to regard him as being quite powerful. And meanwhile, each day, these little pieces of trouble dropped on the floor at Richard Nixon's feet and more and more people noticed it. As the level of regard for Nixon's power dropped, the level of danger for his career rose. At the end, Nixon had not the personal political power of a city councilman. He sat in the Oval Office, but he might as well have been in City Hall, in Dayton.

The ability to create the illusion of power, to use mirrors and blue smoke, is one found in unusual people. They reach their objectives through overstatement or understatement, through silent agreements and, always, the use of language at the most opportune moments.

The night Nixon introduced Gerald R. Ford as his nominee to replace convicted Spiro T. Agnew as Vice President, there were strolling strings and champagne in the White House. The notion was to put Watergate behind us; you have won, you have gotten Agnew, now let us forget about it and go on as before. In the pleasure of the evening, James Lynn, the Secretary of Housing and Urban Development, spoke with Thomas P. O'Neill.

"Tip, did you ever think we'd be standing here in the White House with history being made, the Twenty-fifth Amendment working for the first time. There's probably never going to be another night like it in the country's history."

"Not for about eight months," Tip O'Neill said.

Lynn's mouth opened. Tip O'Neill gave this great street laugh of his and jammed a Daniel Webster cigar in his mouth. James Lynn went away from the night with cement in his stomach. When people around him would say hopefully that Watergate was finished, Lynn would tell them it was not finished. Not anywhere near finished.

* * *

Once, for Richard Nixon, there were only two kids on *The Washington Post* newspaper who were causing trouble. Journalism, no matter how skilled, how brilliant, is a passive trade. Words command only when used by someone in command. Words written by a writer cause little immediate change. The full weight of nearly all the newspapers and nearly all the television had been used for eight years to make horrible the war in Vietnam. The war went on, more intensely at the end than it had at the beginning.

Another threat, another enemy for Richard Nixon now sprang up from another area. A judge, John Sirica. He was painstakingly honest. Lawyers and law professors will point to him forever as a reason for the law triumphing in Watergate; that in the end the actions of no other institution was needed: the law handled the matter. Senator Sam J. Ervin, Jr., thundered about the sanctity of the Constitution and Judge Sirica quietly, decisively applied it. And always, there was the Supreme Court ready to make honest rulings. All of which is beautiful for speeches at a Bar Association dinner or a law-school seminar. Yet all those associated with the law, from Sam Ervin and his committee to John Sirica, crept and probed and yet never took the decisive step, never reached out to grab anyone in the name of the law. The committee subpoenaed. The court ordered. For months Nixon surrendered nothing. Always, he held up the results of the election: 61 per cent of the country voted for him. The Ervin committee said it was sad that the President did not cooperate. The court coughed. The law crumbled in the face of an election certificate. There was no evidence suggesting that Nixon planned the Watergate affair. All he did was enter into a conspiracy to obstruct justice in the aftermath. Where I come from, this is only a misdemeanor. The law says nothing about the true crime committed: that of repeatedly lying to 250 million people. All the law could produce was a minor complaint, and as the time dragged, and time could help Nixon, it began to appear that nobody truly was going to press and attempt to destroy a President for a misdemeanor. For if somebody wanted to treat Nixon as a citizen and apply the law to him, the time element would have been minimal.

Once, in a federal courthouse in Newark, in New Jersey, I saw a businessman, ordered to produce his books as evidence, tell a judge named Whipple that the books were lost. Whipple said that was all right with him; the man could just go in the back there, go into the cells, and sit there until the books were found. The businessman sat in a cell for three days. On the fourth day he was joined by a large gray rat which came out of a crack under the base of the toilet. The next morning, Judge Whipple, busy on the bench reading a motion, heard the doors in the courtroom squeak loudly. Whipple looked up. Staggering into the courtroom, unable to see over the huge pile of blue ledger books he carried, was the partner of the businessman. Your honor, we have just been able to locate the books you requested. Now can my friend get out of jail? This is how it works every place there is a courtroom.

But it did not work this way in the Senate Watergate hearing room and, despite the lore of Sirica, it did not work in his courtroom.

Citizens would have been thrown in the slam for contempt. But the half-royalty of the White House held everybody off. Even when John Dean shook a nation with his testimony, there were only a few who felt anything ever could happen to Richard Nixon. Clearly, then, journalism and the law were not enough to do anything about the crimes of Richard Nixon. But this is only natural. This is a country of men, not laws, and therefore the situation at this point needed a man; a working politician; a professional; a drinking, eating, handshaking member of the Elks, Knights of Columbus, Knights of St. Finbar; trustee of Boston College; Man of the Year 1962; National Conference of Christians and Jews; a director to the United Appeal; a ten-term Congressman who had spent 4000 nights at dinner tables everywhere in the city of Washington. Only a working politician could challenge and erode the one thing Richard Nixon could not afford to lose:

the support of political people. And now, early in the game, so early in the game, Richard Nixon had a new opponent who was a popular politician.

This art which O'Neill pursues, this art of mirrors and blue smoke, is not fraudulent. Rather, it is how all of life works: in politics, life is compressed into a small number of people who spend a short period of time in a circle with a stunted radius. The practice of art can only be done successfully, and for the good of others, by human beings who bring with them a little intelligence, a little wit, a little honor—a seascapist must love an ocean before he can make its movement stand still.

And throughout the quest for justice in the nation in the years 1973 and 1974, Thomas P. O'Neill stood in the full nobility of his profession: a politician of the Democratic party.

As such, the man has no visible means of support. There is no badge, no tool kit, no license that says you are allowed to be a politician. There is only your word: I will do it; I will not do it. And if there is one thing that makes Tip O'Neill so effective in his business, made him so effective against Richard Nixon, it is his belief that a commitment—his word given—is an extension of his religion.

Go to any time in his career, pick out a situation and inspect O'Neill's conduct in it, and always you will see the worth of his word. Go to early 1946, the night a Cambridge politician named Chick Artesani came to Tip O'Neill's house with a skinny young man named Jack Kennedy, whom Artesani introduced as the next Congressman from the area.

"I want you to be with us, Tip," Artesani said.

"Well, I'm delighted to meet you, Jack, but I'm sorry I have to tell you and my old pal here that I'm already committed to Mike Neville."

O'Neill had served in the state legislature with Neville for eight years, and O'Neill's word of support for this particular Congressional race had been given to Neville some time back.

Artesani shrugged, Kennedy and O'Neill shook hands, and the meeting ended. When the primary race for the Congressional seat began some weeks later, O'Neill went out onto the streets with Mike Neville. He toured his district, Russell Street, Orchard Street, Blake Street, and rang doorbells and chatted with people.

"Hello, I'm Tom O'Neill. I'm a member of the state legislature and I see you're new in the neighborhood here, and I haven't had a chance to meet you yet. I just want to say I've lived here in the neighborhood thirty-odd years and I'm not busy in the legislature at this moment because the legislature is not in session. So I'm just coming around to point out to you, if you don't mind, that I think Mike Neville will make a great Congressman from this area; he'll give us the type of voice in Washington we deserve. I hope you'll give him your consideration when you vote on primary day."

And the woman he was speaking to excused herself and went to the dining-room table and brought back a pamphlet with a picture of a PT boat on the front. "Is your Mr. Neville running against this brave young Kennedy?"

Tip shook his head and went on to the next house. And then he began to work the people he knew. He came into Mrs. Murphy's house on Orchard Street, and she took him by the arm and led him into the kitchen for a cup of tea.

"Tip, how are you?"

"Well, Nellie, I'm just great. I just came in to say hello. I'm running again for re-election as you undoubtedly know, but I don't have any opposition, so I want to come here and talk to you about Mike Neville . . ."

Nellie Murphy said, "You don't have any opposition? Isn't this young fellow Kennedy running against you?"

"No, Nellie, he's running for Congress in Washington against my friend . . ."

"Oh, thanks be to God, Tom, I thought he was running against you. What a wonderful boy. We've got all this literature. Oh, what a beautiful story about the PT boat, getting lost in those islands. Dear God, I don't know how I could have voted even for you against such a wonderful, brave young man."

When O'Neill got home that night, there was a phone call from candidate Mike Neville.

"What are you doing?" Neville asked.

"I'm taking a shower and you better do the same thing," O'Neill said.

As the campaign went on, Chick Artesani called O'Neill again. "I'm with Mike Neville, and that's it," O'Neill said. Jack Kennedy then called. The answer was the same.

One night, a next-door neighbor, Joe Healy, called O'Neill. "I've got Jack Kennedy here and I'm bringing him over to see you."

"Don't bring him here, it'll only embarrass him, and you'll embarrass me too," O'Neill said. "I'm with Mike Neville and that's it."

"Kennedy is going to win," Healy said.

"That doesn't have anything to do with it," Tip said.

A few minutes later the doorbell rang. It was Healy and Kennedy. O'Neill stood in his living room and said, "There's nothing I can do for you, Jack, I'm with Mike all the way."

From O'Neill's house, Healy and Kennedy went up to the home of Leo Diehl, O'Neill's closest friend. Diehl was delighted and flattered by the young Kennedy's attentions. But there was no way he could help. "I gave my word to Neville," Leo said.

On primary day, wherever Tip O'Neill looked, he saw coming down off the porches of their frame houses, coming down to vote, hundreds of housewives with pictures of PT boats in their hands.

The day after the election, the first phone call Tip O'Neill received was from Jack Kennedy. "Tip, I want you to know that the next time I do anything, I want you to be with me. When you have a friend, when Mike Neville had a friend like you, a trustworthy friend, then I want you to know I appreciate the position you were in and I will never forget how you acted."

* * *

And in 1974, when it all began in Congress against Richard Nixon, most politicians did not want to hear of impeachment. What is this impeachment? Freak John Dean, who elected him? What the hell does a courtroom have to do with our business? Let the judge go out and run for office. We're elected officials. If you can impeach Nixon, then you can impeach any of us. Translated into newspaper stories, this became a cry for national stability. But when a Tip O'Neill began using the word impeachment on the floor of the House of Representatives, this changed the issue. For he was no frivolous dreamer from the West Side of New York. This was a bone politician, a man with a word, and he gave great believability to the prospects of impeachment merely by saying it.

And this, Richard Nixon could not stand. He was too removed, too isolated, to watch the mirrors being arranged and the blue smoke rolling over them. You can't play baseball unless you get a baseball field and play baseball. Richard Nixon could not play politics if he was not going to be in the room where they had the smoke machine going. The game therefore began in his absence, and you had this first quiver, not a shudder, just this slight quiver, which ran across the floor of the House of Representatives. Something was happening. But you had to be there to feel the vibration on your feet.

* * *

39

In June of 1973, when John Wesley Dean III slipped into the witness chair at the Senate Watergate hearings, among those watching television closely was Jerome Zeifman. Zeifman's original suspicions hardened: Dean admitted a number of illegal acts; it followed that Nixon was involved in each of them. Zeifman saw O'Neill.

"Mr. O'Neill, there is one thing you ought to know, Nixon has committed a variety of crimes."

At the time, most people seemed to see it as a matter of John Dean's word against the word of the President of the United States. And that while a majority of the public might believe John Dean, there was general agreement that this still was hardly enough to ignite Congress into impeachment.

Tip O'Neill saw it differently. Steinbrenner alone had been enough justification for O'Neill to consider impeachment. With Dean's testimony in front of him, O'Neill couldn't see how much more was needed. Not being a lawyer, he was stuck with his good sense, which told him that Nixon was through.

* * *

At the end of July in 1973, Congressman Robert Drinan sat in his office late into each evening, hair matted with sweat, blue eyes concentrating on the piles of papers about him. He was preparing a resolution for the impeachment of Richard Nixon. This one was different. He was not using mirrors and blue smoke. He was using logic and reason and right. Which is why the impeachment resolution was not only ludicrous, it was dangerous: it could screw up the serious work that was already being done. The bill would have lost badly, with damaging public effect. They refer to Drinan as the Mad Monk. He is a Jesuit law professor out of Boston College and was one of the leaders of the antiwar movement. A McGovern man. What more do you have to say? Drinan also happens to be a brilliant law professor. His resolution called for Nixon to be impeached over the Cambodian war. But, shrewdly, Drinan did not take up the issue of whether the war was wrong or not. He called for Nixon's impeachment on the basis that Nixon should have informed the Congress that he was conducting a war in a country called Cambodia. As evidence of Nixon lying to Congress on this matter, Drinan had this quote from April 30, 1970: "We have scrupulously observed the neutrality of Cambodia for the last five years." Drinan then showed that over 3700 bombing raids had been conducted over Cambodia.

Word of Drinan's resolution reached Carl Albert, who immediately called in O'Neill. Albert pointed out the danger to all their hard work represented in Drinan's proposal. O'Neill spoke to Drinan. There was, of course, no way to talk Drinan out of it.

O'Neill took one last stab. "Well, you know, it's a little premature."

The use of the word surprised Drinan. He looked it up in the dictionary. The definition was "coming a bit ahead of its time, a premature time."

Drinan told himself that he had touched a nerve end with his idea. He informed other people of the use of the word "premature." More mirrors were moving.

On July 31, 1973, Drinan stood on the floor of the House of Representatives and began. "Mr. Speaker, with great reluctance I have come to the conclusion that the House of Representatives should initiate impeachment proceedings against the President."

An impeachment resolution is a privileged resolution—it must be heard and voted on. Upon Drinan's speech, Carl Albert hurriedly called Tip O'Neill over.

"The floor must be guarded at all times," Albert said.

"Absolutely," O'Neill said.

"One of us has to be here at all times," Albert said.

41

A Republican could move at any time to have the Drinan resolution brought up for vote. At this time, the most votes an impeachment resolution could possibly get would have been twenty-five. Such a vote would appear in the newspapers as a vindication of Nixon by Congress.

"That would have been very bad psychologically," Carl Albert explained.

So each day, from noon until 7:30 and later at night, either Albert or O'Neill or Whip John McFall sat on the House floor, sometimes with only fifteen others present, in order to prevent any sudden Republican move on the Drinan resolution. Albert and O'Neill had agreed that the Democratic move would be to vote to have the resolution tabled. But as they took turns standing guard duty each day, they became tired. It was late in the year for Congress, they were heading for an adjournment, and the house dragged particularly slowly. Finally, O'Neill ambled around the chamber to speak to Jerry Ford, the Minority Leader.

"Jerry, you know the walls have ears around here, and I've heard that some of your people want to bring this Drinan resolution up for a vote. Is that so?"

Ford said, "Tip, I've checked with the White House on that. They said it would be foolish for us to force a vote now. Somebody would just put up another resolution tomorrow. It's not the most important thing in the world for us."

"Thanks, Jerry."

O'Neill left the floor smiling. He now had some freedom of movement. And he also had established on the floor of the House this little bit of tension. The word impeachment had been in the room, not as part of a move by the lunatic Left, but as part of the normal business conducted by the Democratic leadership. Of course there were only twenty-five votes in favor of it right then. But what the hell, how many people had been exposed to the smoke? One other item of the day comforted him. Ford had not seemed distressed by the topic. He listened to the White House. Obviously they were not even regarding the possibilities of impeachment.

3

"He never even told his own family."

* * *

Tip O'Neill lives at 26 Russell Street in North Cambridge, the part of Cambridge where people do not go to Harvard. He lives three houses away from the two-family house in which he was born. The house is a gray three-story house on a block with houses that are scarred from the years, a block that has a driveway entrance to Salvi Ford Sales and, down at the corners, the Cambridge Nursing Home, the Veterans of Foreign Wars post, and the Di Anthony School of Hairdressing. A couple of black families live on the block. The cab driver taking you there slaps the dashboard as the dispatcher's voice snarls over the radio, "Junior, don't you yell at me no more over the radio or you'll be sorry." In a lunch counter on the main street, Massachusetts Avenue, the waitress stands behind the counter shaking her head about her boss. "He'll give me," she says to the painter at the counter. "He'll give me all right. He'll give me, he'll give me drachmas. No, that's Greek. What is it in Italy they give you? Christ, it's the same thing, anyway. He'll give me nothin'." It is here at places like the Star Market, and with constituents like Red Fitzgerald, that Tip O'Neill's life and career are one.

Two miles away on Massachusetts Avenue begins the part of Cambridge where Harvard rules. Old red brick, old trees, old ivy, and old attitudes about the people in government who look like O'Neill does. At six-foot-two, and weighing anywhere from two hundred sixty-two to two hundred eighty-two pounds, with a great nose, Tip is not trim enough, nor does he have the outward elegance to cause people to use Latinate words in describing him. "I have an agreement with John Kenneth Galbraith," Tip says. "I don't say anything bad about him, and he doesn't endorse me in election years." But O'Neill knows Harvard. And he knows Radcliffe and Boston University and Suffolk Law and Massachusetts Institute of Technology and Boston College and the other schools in his district, the Eighth Congressional District of Massachusetts, an area with the greatest concentration of schools and students in the nation. Tip O'Neill lists over 100,000 students and teachers as constituents. Just as he does not have to be told what the waitress on Massachusetts Avenue believes, while she gropes for the word "lire," he also does not have to be told where Derek Bok of Harvard or John Silber of Boston University stand on an issue. And by this time, by the summer of 1973, Tip O'Neill knew it was right to be calling for an impeachment investigation of Richard Nixon. And he also knew it was not going to hurt him a bit in his district to have the matter go all the way through. There were no meetings at Harvard to pressure Tip O'Neill. Raoul Berger never cornered him over sherry and implored him to act. O'Neill's race-track instincts had him there ahead of all of them. But through the months that were to come, when he would become known as one of the strongest people in Washington pushing for impeachment, Tip O'Neill would always be able to turn the mirror if he felt like it and have people see that he had no other choice; it wasn't personal, it was a matter of serving the people of his district, reacting to them, surviving as a politician.

* * *

There were many people and many forces responsible for the end of Richard Nixon in the summer of 1974. It is difficult to determine which set of men and circumstances were most responsible. The full story will never become altogether clear in our time. Who becomes famous so often depends upon the politics of the academic world years later. Some historian will gain access to bundles of dusty letters, and the historian promptly announces that the author of the letters is a great force in history. He will receive the Sumner Prize for Originality. It usually matters not how much actual value the man had in his time.

The historian can produce the legend and the supporting evidence, and tell it throughout the academic world. In the small of the night, working with his subject, beginning to live with a man he never saw and knows only through letters and other papers, the historian naturally begins to make his subject larger and to prove his theme of how crucial the personality was to great events of history. There was a back-room politician in the Whig party named Thurlow Weed, who was active in the 1830s to 1850s, active as far as the records show. Thurlow left great batches of letters extolling himself and all that he said he had done. The letters were discovered over a hundred years ago by Glyndon Van Deusen, University of Rochester, who proceeded to write a full-length biography of Thurlow Weed.

There should, however, be no difficulty in placing O'Neill. He appears to have done the most to gather and pack together the first particles of the bureaucracy, the particles squeezed together so tightly that pressure forced them to tumble over each other, tumble forward in the granular motion of a glacier. A bureaucracy under way, just as a glacier, does not halt upon command or obstacle. The bureaucracy takes on a life of its own and determines its own finish. O'Neill, who was the first to start the bureaucracy off, the first to see its initial imperceptible motion, also became the first to foresee its result. In October of 1973, when all available experts counted one hundred twenty-five votes at most against Richard Nixon if impeachment ever came to the floor of the House, O'Neill sat over Sunday brunch on Cape Cod and assured family and friends that the votes would be there.

Weighing as much as he does, O'Neill does not look like a figure who has had anything to do with history. The thinness, the austerity, and the haughtiness that glare at you from oil portraits of such men is totally absent in O'Neill. He comes with the full blood of Cork City in his face. A great head of silver hair allows O'Neill to be picked out of a crowd at a glance. He has a large bulbous nose that is quite red. Large blue eyes sometimes seem to be sleepy-slow and have led a thousand victims into thinking that they were on the verge of winning. When he has a thick Daniel Webster cigar stuffed into one corner of his mouth, O'Neill appears to be a backroom politician who always has a drink or a contract in his hand. Someday, when he gets very old, I think O'Neill might say that no matter how far he went in life, how powerful he became, this appearance, as interpreted by so many others, prevented him from going even further, from going to the places where his talents belonged. Because if you see in a man and say of a man only that he is a big, overweight, cigar-smoking, whisky-drinking, back-pounding Boston politician, then somewhere over the years the man himself, somewhere deep down under the winces, could begin believing some of this himself and his momentum would become diminished. In this case, the Protestant ethic has robbed us of our eyes. For if you see Tom O'Neill as he is, not as conformity forces us to see, then there is coming into the room a lovely spring rain of a man.

He is not gruff; he is courtly. He is not cunning; he is open. His choice of words and the rhythm with which he uses them are many levels above most people who are great successes in private and public life. He does not become mesmerized with the sound of his voice; he is a spectacular aural learner.

However, he most certainly is one of those old-fashioned politicians that most people prefer to detest. So much of his life has demanded caution, waiting in line behind others, that he can often make going along sound like accomplishment. In 1967, speaking at Boston College, he told a crowd why he was in favor of the nation's policy in Vietnam: "I've been briefed forty-four times by the President, the State Department, the CIA, and the Department of Defense," he said. "I know more than you." He then went into the light-at-the-end-of-the-tunnel speech. A student named Pat McCarthy stood up and asked one question: "You've been briefed by the people in favor of the war. Have you ever been briefed by the people on the other side of the question?" O'Neill was shot down by the question, and he knew it. He began to go around asking second-level Pentagon and CIA people about the war. They told him it was a disaster, that the country was being lied to. In August of the same year, in the 150,000 copies of his newsletter to constituents, O'Neill came out against the war. He informed no one else of it, however. It wasn't until October that *The Washington Star* heard about it and printed the story. That night, Lyndon Johnson had Secret Service men pull O'Neill out of a card game. Johnson asked O'Neill why he had done it. O'Neill said because he felt everybody was lying, even to Johnson, about the way the war was going. "Well, I've got one request of you," Johnson said. "Just don't go around giving interviews about it."

"Why?" O'Neill asked.

Johnson then leaned on old friendships. He said that O'Neill had been allowed into Sam Rayburn's old "Board of Education," that John McCormack was the one who had brought him into such an inside society. Somehow, Johnson saw this as an obligation. Somehow, O'Neill saw the same thing. He left the office and did not become one of the major voices against the war. His instinct might have taken him to the right decision, but his talent was betrayed by the life he had lived. Which makes his actions against Richard Nixon all the more important. We leave his full career for others to evaluate. Much more important is that here, in this single rare instance, O'Neill, and all these other politicians we scorn, stood up, stood apart from their pasts, and took us to heights we as a nation never have seen before.

* * *

Because of this, I decided to spend the summer of 1974 in Washington, in the office of the Majority Leader of the House, and watch the daily picture that would reflect and suggest the whole of what was going on. At the same time there would be as both company and subject a participant in the impeachment who had all the things that were missing so badly from the whole. In a time of lies and fear and weakness and hypocrisy, in a time when evil was matched against evil and the results were pronounced as good, O'Neill provided a few shafts of sunlight, of charm and humor and mature compassion. Nobody ever said you have to torture life to produce history.

We are not going to learn what happened to the Administration of Richard Nixon for many years; those who would attempt to tell the story now are only frauds in search of hasty profits. But from the bits and pieces gathered over a summer, from what was seen and heard, some important impressions were drawn. Many people feel that Republican politics in California—twisted, religiously negative—is responsible for much of Nixon's personality. Perhaps. And all the more reason to tell of real politicians on the other side, who are involved in a hard business, a devious business, but a business that still tries to work for people instead of against them. The people who come from real politics, from the politics with a tradition of a Boston (supposedly the rowdiest in this country), have qualities that should be examined before anybody from another area, from a California, is allowed to use his business as an excuse for his tactics.

O'Neill, one of the first to call for impeachment, was, at the end, the only man I knew who felt that Gerald Ford was correct in pardoning Richard Nixon. On the Sunday afternoon of the pardon, O'Neill was in a hall in Cambridge. With the crowd calling for blood, O'Neill stood in the back and said to Walter Sullivan, the Mayor of Cambridge, "I don't want to ask you where you stand, but it looks to me right now like I'm the only vote in the place in favor of the pardon."

Secular writers would make a mess of this, as they made a mess of most of the reports on the demise of Richard Nixon. For it takes a belief in, and some comprehension of, Original Sin before you can see enough of Richard Nixon to both remove him and then ask that he be attacked no more. Original Sin is a cruel and vicious doctrine, subscribed to mainly by conservative members of the Catholic Church, but a doctrine which at this time appears needed by all human beings. For a belief in Original Sin is constant acknowledgment of the dark side of man. Born with it, he walks with a darkness always in his nature. The Catholic form is to search for forgiveness of Original Sin, and for a means to control it over a lifetime, through the Grace of Confession. These ceremonies of

the religion—the Confession, the liturgical services—
form a third-party intermediary; but with no way to
externalize his evil, Nixon had only himself. Therefore, with no outward doctrine calling for the continual
planning for failure, for sin, Nixon was unprepared for
failure. Always, secular writers point out that Richard
Nixon was a born loser and that he continually acted
as such. This theory is in opposition to reality. Nixon's
true fault was that he had no way to plan for failure,
no way to externalize his evil.

In the 1970s, there are nuclear physicists who write
of uncertainties, of indeterminate action, all coming
from complicated third-party actions. In trying to understand this, in chasing the notion, they are merely
drawing abreast of ancient religious writings which
called for man to externalize his sin, his evil, to establish a third-party intermediary.

It is depressing that Nixon never dealt with any of
this. Despite all the hysteria, he is not particularly different from anybody else. To look at him objectively,
as now you must, is to understand that Richard Nixon,
not the Kennedys, is the greatest American story—he
ranged the furthest, from grocery store to world
leader, and he ended in enormous, self-inflicted trag-
edy. Keeping his evil internal ruined him. With him
being judge and jury of his own sins, a self-hatred was
produced, resulting in continual accusations against
others: "Nobody drowned at Watergate." A jury decision in a case against John Ehrlichman was a "blot on
the criminal justice system." He twisted everything into instruments of revenge: send draft evaders to prison
in the name of those who died in the war. If he had
had a method of externalizing his evil he would have
had a somewhat better chance against the life he led.
It does not cure to externalize, but it provides for a bit
more mercy, a little more ability to face the truth.

On the day that Richard Nixon left the White
House, stepped into the helicopter on the lawn, and
was gone forever, one of his chief defenders in the fi-

nal months, Dean Burch, went home and had a drink. "He never told me the truth about the thing," Burch said. "He never even told his own family. That was why they were fighting so hard right to the last minute. They were the last to give in on resignation. They thought he was being screwed. He never told them the truth. I think that was his major failure, being so cynical. The man didn't believe in anything. He didn't believe in a religion or principle of anything. He was totally cynical."

* * *

This cynicism is one reason why Nixon had his taping system.

Late one day, on one of the last days of the summer's travail, O'Neill came into his office and watched the evening news on television. He almost never sees the news on television, weekends once in a while, but for the past few days the set had been on constantly. The newsmen on this night were talking, again, of Nixon's tapes.

"I'll tell you a story about these tapes," O'Neill said. "Say, I'll have Canadian Club and Fresca, I'm on a diet. Thank you. Now, the night the Vietnam war ended, Nixon had a few of us over for dinner before he went on television to tell the country that there was a peace agreement. We were over in the Executive Office Building. They have a beautiful place there. There was Nixon, Kissinger, Mansfield, Scott, Griffin, Rhodes, Byrd, and myself. We got there at six thirty and we had a couple of drinks. Nixon was to go on television at nine. At seven o'clock we sat down to eat. Naturally, we all were talking over dinner about the end of the war, and I had a question to ask. I said, 'Mr. President, I'm not going to address this question to you. I don't want to embarrass you and have you give an answer that perhaps you don't want to. So I'll address this question to Henry Kissinger. My question is: you ended the war by bombing Hanoi and mining Haiphong harbor. I happen to have been very close to Lyndon Johnson and I heard these same tactics discussed many times. Bombing of Hanoi and the mining of Haiphong harbor. But President Johnson could not get an off-the-record agreement with Russia and China, so he was afraid that if he did combine the bombing of Hanoi and the mining of Haiphong harbor it might end up with World War III. Five years later, we bomb Hanoi and mine Haiphong and the war is over. Therefore, you must have had an agreement with Russia and China that allowed you to do it."

"And Nixon says, right away, 'Henry, I'll answer that question. I'll take this one myself.' And then Nixon says, 'There was no implied agreement with Russia and China. No implied agreement that allowed us to bomb Hanoi and mine Haiphong harbor. The President made this decision himself. It was the President who decided it had to be done, that it was worth the risk to end the war. There was no implied agreement with Russia and China.'

"As he's saying this, he first has raised his voice. Then I see he's looking upward, at the chandelier or whatever was there. 'No implied agreement with Russia and China. The President made this decision himself. It was the President who decided.' Now I see he's not only looking up but he's pointing with his finger, as if he's talking to somebody up there. And I say to myself, You've got to be kidding. He has this place bugged. So now that night is over. That's in January of 1973. Later that year, in October, the Israeli war ended and the President had us over to his office in the White House to tell us about how the war came to an end and what it was to mean. Remember, he had no tapes going this time. The tapes had been discovered back in July and the system had been taken out. So now Nixon is sitting there, with no tapes going, and he says that the major obstacle had been the Russian propaganda machine in the Middle East. The peace settlement couldn't have been made without the help of the Russians. Nixon said, 'We needed their help. It was the same with Vietnam. We couldn't have done anything unless we had been able to make an agreement with Russia and China before we went ahead at the end.' I'm taking down notes while he's talking and I just say to myself, Oh, boy!

"Now that tells you what he was going to do with those tapes. He was going to take them with him when he left and spend years editing them, and then he could string together a record of his own which would show that he was the greatest man ever to live. He'd be able to prove it with tapes. You never would have known about any of the other stuff. That would have been thrown away. They would have only given you all these tapes with him making a hero out of himself. 'There was no implied agreement with Russia and China. The President made this decision himself.' "

"There is," wrote Kierkegaard, "no temple-robber, toiling in shackles of iron, so vicious as those who pillage among sacred things; and even Judas, who sold his Master for thirty pieces of silver, is not more despicable than those who traffic in great deeds."

* * *

On September 25, 1973, at 3:45 p.m., Carl Albert, Speaker of the House of Representatives, waved to O'Neill, who came to the rostrum.

"I've just received a call from the Vice President. He said he wanted to see me at four. He'll be in my office. Will you be here?"

"I'll be right here," O'Neill said.

At 4:10, one of Albert's aides came onto the floor and told O'Neill that he was wanted in the Speaker's office. The aide then went over to the other side of the chamber to find Jerry Ford.

O'Neill and Ford walked into the Speaker's brown-tiled office to find Spiro Agnew sitting stiffly, tensely waiting for them. Secret Service agents moved in and out, ear radios squawking.

"The Vice President has a matter he'd like to discuss with you gentlemen," Albert said.

"My problem, gentlemen," Agnew began, "is that in Baltimore we have a young United States Attorney named George Beall. He is mean and ambitious. His father was my great friend. This young man would not even have his own job today if I had not gone along with it. The father would be spinning in his grave today if he knew what the son was trying to do to me. I helped get this boy his job and here he is harassing me."

O'Neill remembered that he knew the father, former United States Senator Glenn Beall. O'Neill had been introduced to Beall by Paul Dever, the former Governor of Massachusetts. The meeting took place when O'Neill first came to Washington, in 1952. They were all together in Maryland politics, the Bealls and Agnew, O'Neill reminded himself. He does this all the time, goes over the players. He is a man who likes a score card at all times.

"I am being framed and harassed over campaign contributions," Agnew said. "I am clean. I have nothing to hide. But with this Beall, the way he is going about it, why, gentlemen, no politician living in the greater Washington area is safe. Let me explain what he is doing to me."

Agnew started outlining what he thought were new immunity provisions of the criminal law put together by John Mitchell. Actually there had been no change. Federal law gives a person immunity for testifying in a case only for those facts the person himself deals with. If the government can prove by independent sources that the person is involved in the same crime, the immunity does not protect the person. Agnew told the people in the room that this new immunity law was designed to help the government break up narcotics rings. Now, horror, it was being used against him.

Agnew read part of the letter which said there were great Constitutional precedents, involving the case of John C. Calhoun, which made it impossible for a President or a Vice President to be criminally tried in court while in office. He was absolutely certain of this as he spoke. O'Neill is not a lawyer, so he is unencumbered with such certainties. *What the hell ever happened to "No man is above the law"?* he thought. Agnew also said he was turning over in the morning all materials and records applicable to his case. He would send them to the Clerk of the House.

"If all these people being offered immunity by Beall were telling the truth, then I'd be a rich man," Agnew said. "This Beall is inviting people to come in and build a case against me. People that I never saw or even heard of are being offered immunity. Now, gentlemen, as Vice President I am presenting to the House, delivering by hand to the Speaker now, a request in writing for the House to make an inquiry into my case. I request that my matter be turned over to the Judiciary Committee for a complete investigation, an open investigation, gentlemen, on television, so I can prove my innocence to the people of the United States. Gentlemen, I am being robbed. My life, my career, my family, we are being threatened by young zealots. My God, I don't want to be the first Vice President of the United States indicted for a felony. It is unconstitutional for them to do it. But I have no chance against these young zealots. They will do anything to destroy me. Destroy us all. I don't know whether it is out of jealousy or insanity. But they are ready to do it to me. I will be ruined forever, and the name of my family ruined forever. I ask, I implore you for help."

While the words were deferential, his attitude was not. Haughtiness came out of him as he sat there, stiffnecked, slick-haired, smoldering eyes. But voice throbbing, he had touched a common chord. They were of a trade, politics, which places everything on the word survival. And here was Agnew, a fellow politician, whose survival was threatened. And threatened by the one subject with which they were all too familiar, campaign contributions.

Albert decided that more people had better hear the story. He asked for Majority Whip John McFall, Les Arends, the Minority Whip, and Lew Deschler, who at the time was the House Parliamentarian. When they arrived, Agnew again told his story. As he was telling it, the door opened, and Albert's aides placed more chairs in the room. Barry Goldwater and Hugh Scott arrived; the hallway outside Albert's office was crowded with reporters and cameramen. It was decided by everybody in the room that Albert would go to the rostrum, read Agnew's letter, and take no action. On the floor at this time, a debate over an immigration bill was taking place. Albert walked into the pale light of the chamber, indicating the debate should halt.

"I have a communication from the Vice President of the United States," Albert said. He read the letter.

" 'I respectfully request that the House of Representatives undertake a full inquiry into the charges which have apparently been made against me in the course of an investigation by the United States Attorney of Maryland.

" 'This request is made in the dual interests of preserving the Constitutional stature of my office and accomplishing my personal vindication.

" 'I cannot acquiesce in any criminal proceedings lodged against me in Maryland or elsewhere, and I do not look to any proceedings for vindication.' "

Precedents involving Calhoun, bits and pieces of used hocus-pocus assembled into legal language by lawyers without a case. The letter ended with Agnew saying, ". . . no grand or petit jury could fairly consider this matter on the merits. I therefore respectfully call upon the House to discharge its Constitutional obligation. I shall of course cooperate fully. As I have said before, I have nothing to hide."

Albert walked off the rostrum and returned to his office.

Tip O'Neill said, "I think the Vice-President should be allowed to leave now so that we can discuss the matter."

Agnew rose and left. The room was tense because of him. It was one thing to say, with ease, that Agnew had done something and thus had to be removed. But Spiro Agnew also had run on a ticket elected by one of the largest margins in history, he was a man with a great natural constituency, a group powerful enough to gain for him the Republican nomination for 1976. Nobody plays light with these circumstances.

Albert immediately sent for Peter Rodino and Edward Hutchinson, the senior Republican on the Judiciary Committee.

Ford, Arends, and Hutchinson took over the conversation. Ford said he felt great sympathy for Agnew, and he thought the House should proceed with his request. Hutchinson and Arends agreed. Scott and Goldwater nodded. Ford then went on to discuss the method of taking the Agnew matter to the Judiciary and also the public hearings on television. Perhaps somewhere, in old high-school papers in East Grand Rapids perhaps, the record might show Gerald Ford as taking a stand on the merits of a matter, rather than on interests special to him. Perhaps there is a record of such a thing happening. So far the record is not to be found in his long, bland career in Washington.

O'Neill made notes on a small pad during the conversation. The letters grew larger as he scrawled, in agitation, that the Republicans were speaking as if the matter had been settled. If they allowed Agnew to bring his case into the House, the matter would take months. A year. And where would this leave them with Richard Nixon? For months now, O'Neill had been telling Albert and Rodino that an impeachment of Richard Nixon was going to hit the House and they had to be ready for it. How were they ever going to handle the Nixon matter if the House, the people, the machinery were groping through the matter of Spiro Agnew?

The ready smile, the quick warmth, the fellowship were gone when O'Neill stopped writing his notes and looked up and said, "I don't go along with this at all. We're Democrats and we're in the majority. Now, Jerry, why don't you people go to your office and we Democrats will stay here and discuss this thing. For, frankly, I'm bitterly opposed to this right now."

The Republicans—Scott, Goldwater, Ford, Arends, and Hutchinson—left. Remaining in the Speaker's office were Albert, McFall, Rodino, and Lew Deschler. Rodino called for his chief counsel Jerome Zeifman.

As Zeifman came into the office, Albert said to him, "What do you think of the Vice President's letter?"

O'Neill said, "Hey, let him read it first."

Zeifman read the letter. It was a move he had been expecting. Agnew was being represented by Jay Topkis, member of a New York law firm headed by Judge Simon Rifkind, the same New York attorney whose firm was retained by Justice William O. Douglas, when Jerry Ford called for his impeachment. For the Douglas case, Rifkind, who is as nonpolitical as an alderman, wanted full hearings, counsel present and on television, in the House Judiciary Committee. Rifkind's philosophy was that any matter placed in Congress automatically disappeared. Now, as Zeifman saw, Topkis was trying the same strategy with Agnew. Zeifman read the letter and looked up. He of course was against it. He looked at O'Neill. Zeifman knew he had one vote with him anyway.

"I'm against this," O'Neill said. "The matter is before the courts, and Agnew is going to court to get an injunction to prevent the bringing of evidence before the grand jury. Now he says the Constitution protects the President and the Vice President from criminal action. This is what *he* says. I don't know that at all. I think we ought to leave that up to the courts."

The meeting broke up with no decision. It was agreed that there would be a meeting the following morning.

At 9:30 the next morning, O'Neill was in the House restaurant having hash and eggs when Gary Hymel came in to tell him the meeting would be at 10:30 in the Speaker's office. O'Neill finished breakfast and went down the hallway to his office. It was ten o'clock. McFall came in. He said the Speaker was having the meeting at that moment. O'Neill reached for the phone.

"Peter and I have it all worked out," Albert told him on the phone. "But you can come up if you want to."

O'Neill went up the one flight to Albert's office. Albert, at his desk, handed O'Neill a press release stating that the House Judiciary Committee would begin inquiries into Vice President Agnew's conduct.

"No," O'Neill said.

Albert and Rodino asked him why.

"Because the man is lying. He says he's innocent and he's being framed. I don't know about that. I think he's worried about going to jail, but he won't tell you that. He can't tell the truth. If we put this into the Judiciary Committee, we're doing exactly what Agnew wants. He'll have this stalled and delayed for so long that the court would wind up having no rights in the matter. And another thing, and I can guarantee this, if you let the man get away with this, then the Democratic caucus will skin you alive."

Peter Rodino sided with O'Neill. Zeifman came into the room with Lew Deschler. Deschler spoke up in favor of the House accepting Agnew's request. Deschler is one of those creatures of large government, elected by nobody, yet holding the illusion of power. Deschler began under Sam Rayburn and lasted through the McCormack years. Now he sat in this meeting, conformist, royalty-leaning, he whose power is threatened is to be aided—for mine could be diminished next—and he argued that Spiro Agnew should have his case examined here, in what he regarded as the most important place on earth, the House of Representatives. Here, where old politicians, not young prosecutors, would know how to inspect allegations against the Vice President of the United States.

"I couldn't disagree more," O'Neill said. McFall, Rodino, and Zeifman agreed with him. Albert looked at the press release. His pen began to go over it; go over it and make the words come out that Spiro Agnew's request for an inquiry—the start of a long impeachment process—was being turned down.

One problem was left. At the meeting of the night before nobody had focused on the delivery of Agnew's material, his records, to the House. If Agnew was able to get all his materials to the House, it would be similar to a criminal getting rid of his weapon. Zeifman told Rodino he felt the House should not accept the records. When this was told to W. Pat Jennings, the Clerk of the House, bureaucracy rose to its highest form.

"I can't do this on my own authority," Jennings told Zeifman. "I'm supposed to accept any materials given to me."

Zeifman argued with Jennings. Jennings took the problem to Lew Deschler, and came back to say, "Lew says I'm supposed to accept it. He says that any person has a right to petition Congress, most certainly the Vice President."

Zeifman made it plain that forces larger than Jennings' career were involved. But Jennings, a bureaucrat refusing either to lose face or depart from the rule book, needed a way out.

"Tell him he's sick and he ought to go home for the day," O'Neill said. "He looks a little tired anyway."

Jennings kept his office closed all day.

Agnew now was left for the prosecutors. His chance to take a criminal case and stall it in Congress, as if it were another appropriation to build a bridge, was gone. He told his staff it was O'Neill's fault.

— 4 —

"Peter is the perfect man for this job."

* * *

Early in the morning of October 10th, the Congressional leadership was called in for a briefing by Richard Nixon; the Arab-Israeli war had erupted on the 6th. Those arriving at the White House were tense. O'Neill walked into the Oval Office, nodded hello to Nixon and Henry Kissinger, and sat down. He took out his pad of white paper so he could keep notes.

Kissinger began to explain what had happened. The Arabs, taking advantage of the Yom Kippur holy day, had crossed the Suez and . . .

"Ah . . . we had trouble finding Henry. He was in bed with a broad," Nixon said. He began giggling and rolling his head around.

Kissinger went on with the details.

"Henry, which girl was it that you were with?" Nixon said.

Kissinger kept explaining the war.

63

"It's terrible when you have a girl and the Secret Service has to break in on you," Nixon said. He leered and winked.

On his notes, O'Neill wrote, "President is acting very strangely."

When the meeting broke up, O'Neill rode back to the Capitol with George Mahon of Texas and Thomas E. Morgan of Pennsylvania, the only Congressman who is a physician. Morgan said he thought Nixon was sick. Laughter while others are being killed has a way of being disturbing.

O'Neill walked into his office, saw Bob Healy of the *Boston Globe,* then went up to the floor. A messenger came and handed him a letter. Somebody called to Tip. He put the letter into his pocket while he was talking. When he was finished, he went into the back of the chamber and had a cigar. He was thinking over the morning. Nixon had acted loony. Then he remembered the letter and he opened it. It was from Agnew. The letter said that he had resigned. As O'Neill read the letter, Agnew was on his way to federal court in Baltimore, where Elliot Richardson would ignore equal justice and whisk Agnew in and out in a matter of minutes.

O'Neill's chest was now tingling with excitement and nerves, and it showed in his flushed face when he walked into his office.

"This must be what it's like when history is being made," he said.

* * *

He had dinner that night with Leo Diehl, who is listed as his administrative assistant but is much more than that. He and Tip O'Neill have been together since 1932. Leo Diehl caught polio when he was seven and it ravaged his legs. Thirty pounds of aluminum braces encase his legs. It is terrible work for him to move on crutches. He has a powerful chest, upper arms, and thick shoulders from supporting himself, body swinging in the air; the feet never touch while he works his way on his aluminum crutches. He has fallen and split his face open when he's misjudged curbs. Many times he has tumbled down flights of stairs. Never is anyone allowed to help him up, or even offer a handkerchief to wipe the blood. And he never has done anything but smile once he got up. He has a sharp nose, gray hair, pleasantness in every line of his face, and Massachusetts politics in his blue eyes.

"No wonder Nixon was so happy," O'Neill said to Leo. "He thinks he's free and clear now with this guy gone."

"He thinks," Leo said.

"You know, Leo, if the guy would've said to us, 'Look, I've got a family. I'm afraid of going to the can.' Geez, that's all you have to tell me. I don't want to see any man go to jail. I don't have it in me. Maybe something could have been done for him. Give him some kind of hearing so he could kill a little time and then disappear. But the way the sonofabitch lied to us. And he acted as if it was our duty to believe him. He's got to be kidding. I don't like to be played for a sucker."

At the end of the night, Diehl pulled himself up and headed for the car, body swinging between the two aluminum crutches. They are a hardship, but it has been worse for him. For many years his crutches were made of rosewood. Back in 1944, he worked in an Army accounting office on Commonwealth Avenue in Boston. The officer in charge of the building was a general named Sherman Miles, an old-line Yankee who also was in politics. General Miles went about as if he were in the Ardennes Forest instead of an office building a few miles from his home. Among Miles's trappings were two huge mastiff dogs, which were walked each day by an aide. One afternoon the aide brought the mastiffs to the elevator to take them out for a lunchtime stroll. The elevator doors opened and the dogs rushed on, overjoyed to find Leo Diehl and his two fine rosewood crutches in one corner of the elevator. Immediately, as the elevator went down, one of the mastiffs sniffed the rosewood crutch, then began to turn around. "Get away," Leo said. The dog raised his leg.

"You dirty sonofabitch," Leo Diehl hollered.

Words were too late. The dog was peeing all over the rosewood crutch and all over Leo Diehl's legs.

Diehl put one shoulder up against the wall for leverage. He put all his weight on the crutch the dog was peeing on. The other crutch came around so hard it whirred. Here came the crutch whipping under the animal's raised leg and into the testicles. The animal went up in the air, giving an enormous howl, then flopped down in such obvious distress that the injuries seemed permanent. The general's aide, catatonic, saw himself reassigned to the Battle of the Bulge.

* * *

At the beginning of October 1973, Dwight Chapin announced that if anybody dared bring him in front of the Ervin Watergate committee, he would take the Fifth Amendment. And Jerome Zeifman, his impeachment precedents piled high, asked Rodino if the material could be printed and distributed to Congress. Rodino said this would be regarded as a direct attack upon Nixon. Zeifman had stacks of Calhoun, of Colfax, of Andrew Johnson and the Journal of James Madison. Over the summer he and Don Edwards, member of the Judiciary Committee from California, had gone to London, where Zeifman, catechist at work, sifted the impeachment files kept by Parliament. Before coming home, Zeifman sat in a hotel room for a week, reading the material until his head hurt. Now he shuddered when Rodino announced they would wait.

The amount of annoyance kept rising; on October 5th, the American Civil Liberties Union had called on the House to begin impeachment proceedings. On the 9th, Rodino sent the impeachment material to the printer. All the printing is done by the Government Printing Office located in a set of gloomy brick buildings in the northwest section of the city. It employs 7400 people who work on machines that run from turn-of-the-century, hand-operated linotypes, matrixes jingling through the smell of hot lead, to a silent light blue cabinet, a Linotron Model 1010, one of five in the nation, which sets 1000 characters per second. Copy for the daily *Congressional Record,* running up to 344 pages, reaches the plant after 8:00 p.m. By 6:30 a.m., there are 55,000 sets of copies on Capitol Hill. Jerome Zeifman's impeachment papers reached the printing plant as part of the night's work on October 9, 1973. The report ran 718 pages of the size used in a quality paperback book. It did not disturb the flow of work in the plant that night. Copies of the book, 1500 bound in a tan paperback cover, arrived at the Judiciary Committee on the morning of October 10.

House Document No. 93-7
IMPEACHMENT
Selected Materials

The foreword was by Peter Rodino: ". . . to promote familiarity with a critical point of American Law, I am pleased to transmit this document as a committee print. It is my hope that these materials, some of them previously scattered in select libraries and in some cases out of print for more than a century, will be more readily accessible to members of the Congress and to a larger segment of the American Community."

A copy of the book was placed on the desk of each

Congressman; a loaded gun for use in a duel. When Tip O'Neill came in, he picked up his copy, thumbed it, turned to the last page, saw to his surprise that it was 718 pages long, and announced, "Peter did a hell of a job."

He walked out onto the floor of the House. "Did you see the book Peter put together? Isn't that some job he did? Geez, that Peter is something. What a job he did. Did you see it?"

"I have it in my office, Tip."

"Well, geez, you ought to read it. Peter did the best research on impeachment that's ever been, they tell me. You ought to see the calls I've been getting."

"Who from?"

"All the Constitutional law professors at Harvard. Christ, I'm going to wind up without a copy of the book for myself. The President of Boston College called and asked me and I only had the one and I had it sent to him. We have to get more of these printed."

"It's that good, Tip?"

"Hey, you got to be kidding. It's a fabulous work. Hey, there's Peter now. What a job he did. I want to go over and congratulate him."

There was now a book on impeachment. It wasn't an undefinable topic any more. Now it was right there, in a book, that Congressmen could lift and feel and thumb through. And on the cover it said, "Impeachment." It was 718 pages long. Jeee-zus! Goddam big book! Seven hundred and eighteen pages long. Keeerist! This is gettin' to be important business now.

Nobody read a line of the book, but everybody held it and looked at the last page to see that it was 718 pages long.

On Tuesday, October 23, 1973, representatives of the White House were due to be in court to answer a court order calling for the tapes and other documents to be turned over to Judge John Sirica who would give them to the Watergate Special Prosecutor. This Nixon did not want to do because the tapes would show among other things that he was very guilty. Nixon had at this time a lawyer named Charles Alan Wright, a professor, a scholar from Texas. Wright had done nothing to stop the rumor that he was the nation's most brilliant Constitutional authority. Charles Alan Wright sat in the White House while Elliot Richardson quit and Archibald Cox and William D. Ruckelshaus were fired. Don't think nothin' of it, Professor Wright informed Nixon.

* * *

On Saturday, October 20, while it was all going on, Tip O'Neill was closing up his house at Cape Cod for the winter. The phone started ringing. One caller was Carl Albert, who said he would wait twenty-four hours before doing anything. The newspapers and television became hysterical. O'Neill kept moving wicker in from the lawn. He knew at that moment, there were 434 other guys reminding themselves to take another look at that 718-page book on impeachment that they had received ten days before.

By Monday, October 22, most people who knew Congress assumed there would be an investigation of the Saturday-night firings. Right away maneuvering began by Congressmen who wanted to be a part of any special committee. There were those who wanted to get the President, those who wanted to defend him, and those who simply wanted to be a part of any history that might happen. Which was all normal. It was the other calls concerning the matter which bothered Carl Albert. Industry people were calling him on behalf of Congressmen who wanted to be placed on the committee. Albert says nothing about it, but it is presumed that at least some of the calls were from oil and natural gas people in his home state of Oklahoma. It was obvious to Albert that the White House was behind the calls, a point he made to O'Neill at a morning meeting. A special committee would be best for

Nixon. By custom, the Republicans would be able to name their own members to the committee, in this case men religiously sworn to uphold their own and obstruct all else. There would be no Caldwell Butlers or Tom Railsbacks. Therefore, Albert shut off his phones and told O'Neill that the investigation would be conducted by the Judiciary Committee and that sentiment for any other form must be thwarted. O'Neill walked out of Albert's office and began looking for his people. Already, Bob Eckhardt of Texas was saying that he regarded Rodino as incapable of handling such a major assignment. Eckhardt spoke of Richardson Preyer of North Carolina as a man suitable to run a special committee investigating the conduct of Nixon.

O'Neill ran into another thing out in the halls, the rumors that Rodino somehow was connected to the underworld in Newark, the Mafia, and would be a disgrace to the Congress as chairman of a committee conducting hearings on the President. "Sometimes the minds of men run bad," O'Neill says. "And somebody had to be feeding some kind of nonsense. Somebody from the White House, you can bet your life on that. All I kept hearing about was Neil Gallagher and Hughie Addonizio, and Peter being involved with them."

Cornelius E. Gallagher, a Congressman from Bayonne in New Jersey, who had been convicted of income-tax evasion and was in prison. A magazine story in 1971, pushed by Charles Colson, had pictured Gallagher as a front for gangsters. Addonizio was from Newark. As a Congressman, he had roomed with Peter Rodino in Washington. One day Addonizio announced he was going back to Newark to run for mayor. "Hughie, what the hell are you doing that for?" O'Neill asked him. Addonizio said, "Christ, do you know what the budget for the City of Newark is? Take one per cent of that and I'm going to have something." O'Neill remembers saying to him, "Hughie, you got to be kidding. The game isn't played that way any more." Addonizio shrugged, went to Newark, and not only began stealing but, worse, was caught. At his trial, names of several hoodlums came up. Addonizio was given a ten-year sentence. In the White House on this Monday in October, the normal move was to connect Rodino to Addonizio and Gallagher—and then take the story over to the House of Representatives and try to sell it, just as you sell a transit bill.

O'Neill heard the stories. He also knew about the phone calls Carl Albert was getting from the big money interests on behalf of the White House.

"Peter is the perfect man for this job," O'Neill kept saying. This is known as an official word. He wanted to put this one together in a hurry.

On Monday the House Judiciary Committee also had a regularly scheduled meeting. As Peter Rodino walked up to Room 2141 in the Rayburn Building, shoulders swinging, big thick heels clicking on the marble hallway, he felt excitement. The newspaper reports the next day said that "Whether the discussion of impeachment becomes more than talk depends upon the cautious chairman, Peter W. Rodino, and the equally cautious House Democratic leadership. Of nine committee members contacted yesterday, six said they favored moves leading to impeachment and three said they were opposed." Excellent. Nobody even mentioned the possibility that the Judiciary Committee had not been given the impeachment matter by the full Congress.

On Tuesday, October 23, Charles Alan Wright dressed himself in the Madison Hotel, his mind concentrating on lofty Constitutional principles he would place before the court—issues that turned to glue when you touched them. He would have lawyers, clerks, judges stuck together like wolves in heat for so many months that nobody would know what was going on. Wright did not include Congress in his calculations. Nor had he actually sat down and listened to Nixon's tapes.

The problem was, Washington on this day was like an electric wire downed in a storm, snapping in the high wind, bolts of electricity sizzling and exploding out of its soaking frayed ends. Constitutional principles or not, if Nixon defied the court order—on top of the Saturday-Night Massacre—an authentic accident just might have occurred: rapid history. The White House asked for a delay—from noon until 2:00 p.m. —before Professor Wright appeared before Judge Sirica. When Congress opened at noon, they were waving and calling out for a chance to get up and offer impeachment resolutions. O'Neill called for the matter to be given to the House Judiciary Committee. Throughout the chamber and in the cloakroom, more Congressmen were calling for a special committee to be set up. O'Neill said in his speech on the floor, ". . . to the House Judiciary Committee for speedy and expeditious consideration. The House must act with determined leadership and strength."

Over at the White House, Richard Nixon sat and brooded. He knew two things that his lawyer did not. One, that he, Nixon, was a liar. And, two, the Congress was in a turmoil. Who needed more trouble because of these freaking tapes? Nixon said something which interrupted Professor Wright's preparations. Professor Wright's face got about six inches longer.

At two o'clock Charles Alan Wright walked into Sirica's courtroom. Tall, large, sharp nose, hair slicked back. Watching Wright as he walked, particularly his stride and head carriage, one had enormous admiration for the long hours Wright must have spent in front of mirrors learning to look just like John Wayne. On this day Wright wore a brown suit, lime shirt, and lime tie. He was impressive as hell. Only the moment Charles Alan Wright sat down, his hand went right for the water pitcher. He gulped a paper cup of water, filled it again, and gulped some more. One thing about

John Wayne, even when he was in the middle of it all at Wake Island with the Japs crawling onto him and the sun glaring, even when it was this tough, John Wayne didn't take a drink of water. Next to Wright sat Leonard Garment of the White House staff. Garment ran a hand over his face. Now he ran the hand through his hair. The hand went back to the face again. Garment's entire weight shifted in his chair.

There was a slap on the desk for attention as Judge Sirica came in. There was a bit of red in Sirica's face. His head had this little irritated nod as he sat down. Charles Alan Wright went to the water pitcher. Then he walked to the lectern. Head bowed to the judge, Wright spoke in a low voice. He said that "this President obeys the law." After weeks of high-sounding, confident talk about the separation of powers, Professor Wright was quitting in the pit in front of the judge. At noontime that day with client Richard Nixon, Professor Wright had discovered a thing he never learned about in all his reading of *Marbury* v. *Madison:* when the client is a liar and you believe him, he takes you down with him.

At the end of the day, O'Neill was at a party at the Congressional Hotel, down the street from the Capitol. It was a campaign-fund raiser for Charles Wilson, a Congressman from California. Wilson proudly took O'Neill around the room. When they stopped, O'Neill said to Wilson, "You know, Peter will do a very good job with this."

"If you say so, Tip, anything you say," Wilson said.

Hugh Carey was in the next room, which is the bar of the Democratic Club. O'Neill and I went in and had a drink with him. Carey was then on the strong, influential Ways and Means Committee.

Carey was telling a story about somebody's wife who was flying from Boston to Ireland on a Saturday night and had neglected to bring a passport with her.

"Seamus calls me and says, 'Geez, I got my wife at Logan Airport and they won't even let her on the plane.' So I said to him, 'Well, let me see what I can think up here.' And Seamus says to me, 'Of course, I'm not in any trouble if you don't deliver.' "

"I know just what you did," O'Neill said.

"Sure," Carey said, "I called Gene Krisak."

"That's right, Gene Krisak. He's a good fella."

"And I told Gene, 'Look, this woman has absolutely got to get to Ireland tonight and the plane is due to leave in a half-hour.' And of course you know only on matters of life and death are they allowed to do it. So I said it was absolutely a matter of life and death."

"And you weren't lying," O'Neill said.

"Absolutely not. It was going to be her life if she got to Ireland, and it was going to be Seamus's death if she didn't get there."

"That's good," O'Neill said. "Say, Hughie, we got to have Peter do this."

"Absolutely, we can't give it to anybody else."

"They've got to be kidding if they think they can put it anyplace else," O'Neill said.

"No question," Carey said.

Elizabeth Holtzman came over from her office to have a drink with us. It was more to say hello than have a drink—a Bloody Mary at eight o'clock at night is not drinking. She is a friendly woman, an intense woman. She talked about the people in her office who were going to stay on through the night working on impeachment material. A New York lawyer, active in reform politics, overheard her and cut in with a display of his great knowledge of the phrases and clauses that make up the books on impeachment law. The man would not stop talking. Elizabeth Holtzman listened with great courtesy. Carey made a face. O'Neill cocked his head so he could appear to listen most attentively. The cigar moved from one side of his mouth to the other as the lawyer from New York talked on.

O'Neill reached out and took my arm. "I was just

thinking," he said. "What was the greatest fight you ever saw?"

"Two guys you probably never heard of," I said. "Heavyweights. Joe McFadden and Nino Valdez. They fought in a place called the Sunnyside Gardens around where I come from in New York. Eight knockdowns in six rounds. I never saw anything like it."

"Do you remember when Tony De Marco fought Carmine Basilio?" O'Neill said. "Do you remember that one, do you? Geez, what they did to each other! You must be kidding, you don't remember the fight? Poor Tony, he was from the *Narth* End, you know. I used to see him all the time. Well the poor guy ran out of gas in the last couple of rounds and, geez, this Basilio, what a job he did on him. But until then, I never saw a fight like it in my life."

Then we went to dinner and he talked about Rocky Marciano. He never mentioned impeachment.

* * *

At noon the next day, O'Neill was on the House floor slipping into a seat in the front, then a seat in the back, moving in and out of the cloakroom, going behind the rail to have a cigar. Talking, talking, talking. In two spots he heard the same thing: "Why should we let Rodino get all that national television time? I've been heading up a committee a lot longer than Rodino has. Let's get somebody we know better in there."

O'Neill chewed on his cigar and thought about the argument. Later he got into a conversation with Gillis Vanderbilt (Sonny) Montgomery of Mississippi. On impeachment, Sonny Montgomery had taken his stand and never was to leave it: "Ah'm the first mate on the *Sequoia* and I intend to stay that way." Yet virtually nobody in Congress dislikes Sonny Montgomery personally. In the market place of legislating, he is one of the men you always go to, no matter how opposite his views.

"You know, Sonny," Tip said, "about this impeachment business going to the Judiciary Committee. Don't you think it would be a wonderful thing to give Peter Rodino a chance to finally get a little television exposure? Let people see what a great guy he is. After all these years of being on the bottom, nobody knowing him, wouldn't it be nice to give him his little chance?"

"Sure, he deserves a chance," Montgomery said. "Thing isn't going to go any place, so we might as well give Peter a little publicity." Montgomery would tell this to others. O'Neill went on to somebody else.

At this point, Peter Rodino decided it would be very good to have another meeting of the House Judiciary Committee to discuss impeachment. In going through the envelopes dealing with Mr. Rodino's career, as recorded in the reference library—the morgue—of the Newark *Star-Ledger* newspaper, I came across a yellow clip, the paper falling into pieces between your fingers, which showed that in 1940 an attorney from Newark's First Ward, Peter W. Rodino, candidate for the New Jersey State Legislature, had been endorsed by Mrs. Eleanor Roosevelt. I am told that Mrs. Roosevelt came to Newark on behalf of her husband, and posed for pictures. At which point the young lawyer from the First Ward, Mr. Rodino, came slicing through a wall of people and he stood, beaming, alongside Mrs. Roosevelt. Pictures were taken. When one of the pictures appeared in the Newark newspapers, Rodino said, of course, the picture speaks for itself; he had been officially endorsed by Eleanor Roosevelt. Blue smoke rose high in Newark that day.

And now, thirty-four years later, in the hall of Congress of the United States, Peter Rodino slipped through the doorway into the Judiciary Committee room. As he was going through, Rodino put his hand out and tipped a huge mirror a few degrees forward.

A vote was taken at the meeting which gave Rodino the power to subpoena any agent of the government, and his papers, public and private, for examination by the Committee. The vote was on straight partisan lines. But there had been a vote. What the hell, if they were voting on it already, then they must be in charge. There also appeared in the newspapers at this time a syndicated column by Charles Bartlett which told of how Rodino would handle the impeachment hearings.

Among the first to believe this was Tip O'Neill. He asked Rodino what he was going to do about a counsel for the hearings. That's the first question you ask. Christ, the counsels for big publicity committees have become famous and if you're in politics you want to know who has a chance to become famous. Kill the baby in the crib if you think he'll grow up to be an enemy. Rodino said he was going to bring in a big name from the outside. He ruled out his staff, including Jerome Zeifman. O'Neill went back to his office and began sending Rodino the names of prospects for the job. Rodino said thank you, but did not bite. Others suggested names to him. Rodino took none of them. Days turned into weeks. In November, O'Neill stood behind the railing in the House, smoking a cigar, muttering about the mail and phone calls from his home district. He put the cigar into the brass ash stand and walked onto the floor and sat alongside Peter Rodino.

"Now, Peter, when can we get this counsel and get going on this thing?"

"Well, I have to take my time, I want this done, I want this to be very carefully done."

"Now, Peter, for Christ's sakes, you have to get it done before we go home for Christmas."

Rodino began to talk about his problems. Like any successful politician he has several styles of speech, all of which must be calibrated in terms of how direct he cares to be at the moment. A Rodino answer can run from one word to six pages. For this moment, Rodino chose a long, rambling answer about the proper counsel for such a massive job.

O'Neill cut in. "Hey, Peter, we have to have a guy by Christmas."

Rodino writhed in the seat. "Hey, Tippy! Do you know how hard it is to find a counsel? Look at the names you sent me. Do you know what one of them was? This, this Cronin. He was a disciple of Father Berrigan. They'd kill us if we had a guy like that around."

"I gave you names so you could look at them. You look at one, you get an idea for another. I don't care. We have to get the man by the time this Congress goes home for Christmas."

"You're not a lawyer, you don't understand."

"Hey, I can read the calendar." They sat in the brown leather seats, in the high-ceilinged old chamber, and they talked about getting started on the impeachment of the President of the United States. Neither had a ruling or a license to do what he was doing. They were surrounded by mirrors and fighting with both hands over what each thought he saw in the blue smoke.

It was lunchtime as the two argued. In the White House, Richard Nixon sat alone, as he did every day, in a small sitting room off the main office—the Oval Office—and he had the same cottage cheese and apple that he had every day that he was in Washington. He never deviated. Alone with cottage cheese. The word impeachment had not even been mentioned inside the White House, and it would not be for months. Nixon never thought about it. The cover-up was a necessary, aggravating political job. There was nothing beyond it. To the nation at this time, and even to most of the men prowling the floor of the House of Representatives, impeachment was totally improbable. But Tip O'Neill and Peter Rodino saw it as a thing that was very real. Nothing, O'Neill knew, was as improbable as the way in which the two of them got to this afternoon in November when they could argue about getting rid of a President.

5

"I know one Republican . . . John Doar."

* * *

For Tip O'Neill, his steps to the Majority Leadership began with problems others got into.

On January 12, 1970, in Room 902, United States Courthouse, Foley Square, New York City, Clifford Sanders, foreman of the grand jury meeting in the windowless room, called for a vote. Under consideration on this wet chill day were the possible criminal activities—fixing an SEC case—of Nathan M. Voloshen, a Washington lobbyist, and Martin Sweig, administrative assistant to John McCormack, Speaker of the House of Representatives. A quorum of jurors was present—sixteen of the twenty-three must be seated—and when Sanders asked for a show of hands on whether there should be an indictment against Voloshen, all were raised. He asked for a show of hands on Sweig. Again, all were raised. Sanders pressed a buzzer. Into the room came a short, dark-haired man who in those days always was first taken for a student, or a well-dressed messenger boy. He was an Assistant United States Attorney named Richard Ben-Veniste, and he was learning about crime by politicians, knowledge which would not hurt him four years later. Sanders gave Ben-Veniste the tally. Ben-Veniste watched the indictment placed into the grand-jury log. The grand jury left for home, and Ben-Veniste went downstairs to the fourth-floor offices of United States Attorney Whitney North Seymour. "I want to tell the Speaker about this myself," Seymour said.

After his phone call, the federal indictments of Nathan Voloshen and Martin Sweig were released to the public. Voloshen had backslapped and smiled his way into the company and confidence of Martin Sweig, whose life had been spent as assistant to the Speaker of the House John McCormack. Out of this great friendship between Voloshen and Sweig grew a few small schemes, all of which were conducted over the telephones in the Speaker's office. In an office such as this, in the Capitol Building itself, a telephone trumps a machine gun. Sweig and Voloshen, most unpardonable sin, were caught.

This was the first of two accidents which brought Tip O'Neill to the Majority Leadership of the House of Representatives, to a position from which he could, in 1974, do much to influence the course of a nation. But until you tell the story of the accidents, you cannot properly tell of O'Neill in Washington in 1974.

For the House of Representatives is not an active, thoughtful body. It never acts; it always reacts. Any strong, definite course taken by Congress in the spring and summer of 1974 was a rare instance in the history of the House.

"Nothing would have happened without O'Neill," my own Congressman, Benjamin Rosenthal, was saying one day. "If Hale Boggs was there, as much as I liked him personally I just know that Nixon still would be President. The same thing with Peter Rodino. We never would have had an impeachment vote in the Judiciary if Manny Celler were still in charge."

At the time when Nate Voloshen and Martin Sweig began manning the phones, O'Neill under normal progression of House politics did not seem to have much of a chance ever to get as high as Majority Leader. The Speaker, John McCormack, a wiry, frugal New Englander—"Is the pudding fresh today?"—was perfectly willing to live forever. Majority Leader Carl Albert waited behind McCormack. Third in line was Majority Whip Hale Boggs of Louisiana. Below them, all waiting, all with much strength of their own, were such as O'Neill, Hugh Carey of New York, Morris Udall of Arizona, Edward Boland of Massachusetts, and Daniel Rostenkowski of Illinois.

In the working of Congress—up to January of 1975 —there is no such thing as a man jumping over another. Certainly not for such posts as Speaker or Majority Leader.

As John McCormack explained it to me, "One day, Mr. Sam told me that, 'Someday you're going to be the Speaker of the House.' And I stayed in the House and waited. And then one day I *was* the Speaker of the House. Pray to God that it always will work the same way."

By September the judge in the case was recommending that Sweig and Voloshen go home and get toothbrushes for the trip to Allenwood Prison camp— John McCormack's time was done before he wanted it to be.

He announced he was leaving Congress at the end of his term, in November of 1970. The House elections for Speaker and Majority Leader—House Democrats vote in caucus—would take place in January of 1971. It was assumed that the chain would move smoothly, that Carl Albert would become Speaker and Hale Boggs the Majority Leader. The chain clicked once: Albert was going to have no trouble. Then it clanked and went off track. Hale Boggs had opposition. Morris Udall was going to run against him, as was James O'Hara of Michigan. The main reason they would run against Boggs was Boggs's own behavior over the past year. He took a drink, old Hale did. He once held a press conference that lasted two hours and consisted mostly of him reading from news clippings, the Bible, and from his personal appointments book. When a reporter would arrive, Boggs would rush back to seat the reporter, then resume reading. But when his living was threatened, Boggs shook his head, buttoned his jacket, and went to work. He gave a large party and walked about sober and affable. Udall still seemed well ahead, but in Hale Boggs's office, Gary Hymel carefully went over the list of freshmen Congressmen due to arrive in Washington in January. Boggs began calling them. When the newcomers arrived in Washington, they came around to Boggs's office. Could he help them? The newcomer mentioned some personal problem with finding an apartment or a school for his children. Boggs pressed a buzzer. An aide came in, and Boggs told him to handle the problem. The votes turned the election for Boggs.

In January of 1971, new Speaker Carl Albert and new Majority Leader Hale Boggs sat down and discussed who would be named Whip. The candidates were Hugh Carey of New York and Tip O'Neill of Massachusetts. Carey had bitter opposition from Brooklyn Congressman John Rooney, an important man on the major Appropriations Committee. Rooney was from Red Hook and spoke like it. He considered Carey, who lived on Prospect Park West in Brooklyn, as being "Lace Curtain Irish." It was a bitterness that started long before 1970, 150 years before at least, and it damaged Carey's chances. O'Neill, on the other hand, was liked by everybody and had the mantle of John McCormack still about him. O'Neill was chosen Whip.

Now, in January 1971, Tip O'Neill was the third-ranking Democrat in the House of Representatives.

Fine. But still a long way from the posts from which the illusion of power could be used against Richard Nixon.

In October of 1972, Hale Boggs went to Alaska to assist in the campaign of Congressman Nick Begich. Boggs went this far because Begich had voted against him in the 1970 election for Democratic Majority Leader. The theory of Hale Boggs, and any other politician who has more than a cabbage for a head, is that you immediately try to win over the man who voted against you. Go to any lengths. In this case, Anchorage, Alaska. On the night of October 15, 1972, Boggs, exhausted from a full day's tour of that part of the territory, decided he was not going to punish himself and get up at 7:00 a.m. to catch the commercial flight from Anchorage to Juneau. Begich chartered a private plane. The pilot, Don Jonz, flew down from Fairbanks on the night of the 15th. He called the weather bureau before he went to bed. "Looks like I'm not going to Juneau," he said. When he woke up in the morning, the weather was still bad. Jonz went to the airport anyway. He fueled the plane and taxied over to the terminal. His plane was a twin-engined Cessna 310. The destination, Juneau, was 560 miles to the southeast, a long, tiring flight in such a small plane. Jonz didn't expect anybody to be at the terminal. He was surprised therefore to see Begich and Russell Brown, his administrative assistant, talking forcefully to a tired, thoroughly wary Boggs. There were, Begich said, television commitments in Juneau and the dinner was a sell-out because of Boggs's appearance. Boggs shrugged and got into the plane. Jonz took the plane out to the runway. It was nine o'clock. He had not expected to be flying in the cold, murky weather. But it did not necessarily disturb him. At thirty-eight, Jonz had been flying in Alaska for ten years. "You gotta be willing to cheat the devil," he told people. He wrote an article for a flying magazine which was entitled, "Ice Without Fear." He flew this time without a personal emergency locator transistor. He had left it at home, in Fairbanks. As the plane left the runway, the weary, uncomfortable Boggs looked at the cold rain streaming down the windows.

The plane was heard from once, just before it went through a mountain pass. Then never again. At nine that night Mrs. Lindy Boggs was notified in Washington that her husband was missing. She called Gary Hymel, Boggs's administrative assistant, who was home watching the Monday-night football game on television. They left for Alaska the next day. The military meanwhile put on an exhaustive search—private and military planes spent 3600 hours covering 325,000 square miles. There was nothing.

* * *

On November 7, Tip O'Neill voted in North Cambridge, then slipped off to the airport with Leo Diehl. They flew to Washington. That night, in the Whip's office, they began taking election returns. Thomas Hale Boggs, Jr., and Gary Hymel joined them. Throughout the night, O'Neill made casual calls to friends who had won elections. He also made calls to the new Democratic Congressmen. All the new winners were flattered and some awed by receiving a call in their local headquarters from the House Democratic Whip. As the night went on, O'Neill, Boggs, and Hymel talked about the Majority Leader's position. On Wednesday morning, Tommy Boggs arranged for O'Neill to call Mrs. Lindy Boggs. Tommy Boggs sat next to Tip O'Neill as he spoke to Mrs. Boggs about the post her husband had held. "Well, all I can tell you is that we have to be practical," she said. "If Hale were around here in a similar situation, he'd be about to want to get started."

When O'Neill hung up, Leo Diehl began punching

phone buttons. Three people began to help him place calls to the Congressmen scattered all over the country. Leo knew from the start that it was going to be all right. And Leo was holding Teno Roncalio of Wyoming.

"He's talking to Brademas, Teno, and the second he gets off, I'll put you through."

"Is this for the Majority Leadership?" Roncalio said.

"Yes, it is, he wants to ask for your vote," Diehl said.

"Oh, hell, I'm voting for him anyway. Let me hang up and get off your back. He doesn't have to ask for my vote."

"Yeah, but he's going to ask you anyway," Leo said.

By Wednesday night, O'Neill had sixty-three committed votes. On Thursday, he put together forty-six. On Friday, they came up with eleven more. This gave him a hundred twenty votes. He was one shy of a majority of the Democratic caucus. In New Orleans, Gary Hymel went to a gathering for Mrs. Lindy Boggs at the home of Hale Boggs's brother, Archie Boggs. Congressman F. Edward Hébert of Louisiana was there. Hébert had been the city editor of the *New Orleans States* when Gary Hymel was a reporter. At the reception, Hymel said to Hébert, "Eddie, you always said to call you if I needed something. And I need you now." Hébert listened. "Tell Tip he has my vote," he said. Hymel went to the phone. He caught O'Neill in Logan Airport in Boston. O'Neill got the news at the airport counter that he was Majority Leader of the House. He and Leo Diehl left the airport singing.

Congressman Sam Gibbons of Florida announced that he too would run for Majority Leader. He made no impact and withdrew on December 26. On January 2, 1973, the 93rd House Democratic Caucus reelected Carl Albert as Speaker. Then Sam Gibbons got up and said, "Tip, I am going to tell you something that nobody else in this room can. You haven't got an enemy in the place."

* * *

It came another way for Peter Rodino.

One night in February of 1972, I was starting to fall asleep on the Eastern Airlines 10:00 p.m. shuttle from Washington to New York when a hand grabbed my shoulder and shook it. Standing in the aisle was Meade H. Esposito, the Democratic leader of Brooklyn.

"Hey, where were you tonight, you should have come to the party," he said.

"What party?"

"The party they gave for me. Manny Celler threw a party for me. He had two hundred and fifty Congressmen and Senators come around to meet me. He said I was the greatest political leader in the country. Manny gave it for me in this big room the Judiciary Committee has. You ought to see the size of the room Manny has."

Esposito took a seat. In front of him sat Eugene Gold, the Brooklyn District Attorney. Esposito slapped Gold on the head.

"Look at this guy, I make him District Attorney and what does he do? Arrests two Italians a day and says he's doing his job."

Meade then held up a plaque.

"Here, see what they did for me? They gave me a plaque. That's Manny Celler's work. He has all the Congressmen and Senators give me a plaque for political leadership. Isn't that something?"

Meade held the plaque and looked at it for a full minute. Then he shrugged and put it down.

"One thing about the plaque that's good, it's a small plaque so I can shove it up my ass like I'm supposed to."

"What was the whole thing about?" I asked him.

"This is how Manny runs a campaign," Meade said.

"He gives me a plaque and I'm supposed to make sure everything is all right in his district. He never comes around. Well, what's the difference? I'll take care of things for him."

"He has no trouble, has he?"

"Well, there's some broad says she's going to run against him in the primary or something. You know these freaking broads. Who knows what she wants? It don't matter. How the hell can you run against the Chairman of the House Judiciary Committee? Manny's a national landmark."

* * *

On a morning a month later, I stopped into Woerner's Restaurant on Remsen Street in Brooklyn, just downstairs from Esposito's headquarters, and Meade, in a back booth, waved for me to sit down.

"I don't know what to do, I can't get this freakin' Liz Holtzman out of the race."

"Who is that?"

"The broad running against Manny Celler."

"Well, is it a fight, or what?"

"Nah. Shouldn't be a fight. It's just that this Manny, you know, he never comes around. And I hear this girl, she's got all kinds of young girls running around for her. Indians. Freaking squaws. I've tried to talk her out of the race, but it looks like I can't do it. Maybe Manny better get his ass up here and see some people. That plaque he gave me can't go out and campaign for him."

On March 29, Elizabeth Holtzman, a thirty-year-old attorney, announced she was running in the Democratic primary against Emanuel Celler, eighty-four, the famous Chairman of the House Judiciary Committee.

"As far as I'm concerned, she doesn't exist," Celler announced.

The years had destroyed Celler's ability to see. By

this time he thought of himself as actually holding power, rather than holding the illusion of power.

The next morning, Ms. Holtzman was on the subway platform handing out literature describing Celler's interest in legislation that helped Fishback & Moore, a company he held interest in.

Only 23 per cent of the people in the district voted in the June primary. Elizabeth Holtzman received 15,596 votes; Emanuel Celler had 14,896. By the margin of 610, she was in Congress. The fabled Celler was retired, and in a Washington apartment on the morning of June 21, a virtually unknown Congressman, Peter Rodino of Newark, New Jersey, found he was the next Chairman of the House Judiciary Committee.

The primary election between Holtzman and Celler could be considered one of the most meaningful elections the nation has had. If Celler had won, he would have dominated the impeachment process with the Judiciary Committee, as he dominated everything about the Committee for his thirty years as Chairman. Brilliant but egotistical, he would have been quite abrasive in such a delicate process. Particularly to needed Republican votes. Celler's large private law practice certainly would have been brought up, much more searchingly than Elizabeth Holtzman had been able to do in Brooklyn. For so many years, Celler had regarded himself as both brilliant and above the normal rules. Any detailed accounting of his personal business would have badly damaged the impeachment process in the Judiciary.

One day, while the Judiciary was studying the case behind closed doors, I ran into Celler, coming off a shuttle at Washington. "What do you think of how they're doing?" he said. "They're taking too much time. They're trying to get it bipartisan. That can't be done. The other side is only going to make it a partisan issue at the end anyway. So you might as well just go right ahead and call them on it. What was it

Macbeth said, 'If it is going to be done at all, better it be done right away.' " He was stooped and his legs seemed unsteady. But his voice was strong. He certainly could have run impeachment hearings. But I kept wondering about his idea of shoving the vote down Republican throats. At that moment, Peter Rodino was carefully, delicately, trying to put together the group of Republicans and Southern Democrats that would give him the vote he needed to convince Congress and the country.

* * *

Later that November afternoon, Rodino complained about the pressures to Francis O'Brien, his administrative assistant. O'Brien is small, dark-haired, and with a serious face. He had worked for Mayor John Lindsay in New York; at the time of widespread prison riots O'Brien was assigned to be the Mayor's liaison with police who were lined up at the House of Detention in Kew Gardens, in Queens. The police inclination was to storm the prison. O'Brien's was to wait. In a prison riot, time never killed anybody. The disturbance ended without a death. When the Lindsay term of office was running out, O'Brien, through his brother, and relatives in Newark, found there was a position open on Congressman Rodino's staff: Rodino, Washington and, in the background, possible impeachment of a President. This dictated an energy and enthusiasm in O'Brien which was visible almost immediately to Rodino. Francis O'Brien also had a mother who is Italian, which is not considered a deterrent by Rodino. Now, as O'Brien listened to Rodino complain about his arguments with O'Neill, he kept thinking of one name.

"It must be a Republican," Rodino said.

"I know one Republican," O'Brien said. "John Doar."

On November 20, John Doar was in his office at the

Bedford-Stuyvesant Restoration Corporation on Fulton Street in Brooklyn, in the center of the largest non-white area in the northern part of the country. Doar's phone rang with a call from Abraham Goldstein, Dean of the Yale Law School.

"There's a funny question I have to ask you," Goldstein said. "Would you be interested in being the special counsel to the Chairman of the House Judiciary Committee?"

"Yes, I would."

"Well, that's all I have to ask you," Goldstein said.

"Well, good-by," John Doar said.

He knew enough to go back to his work and not let the possibilities plague him. The Bedford-Stuyvesant, two- and three-story scarred brownstones and ram-shackle wooden houses, rags stuck in broken windows against the winter, sprawls for miles. The Restoration Corporation, private and public money, was an idea of Robert Kennedy when he was the Senator from New York. Restore entire blocks, with local labor, and have the streets stand there as an example and inspiration for what can be done in the ghetto if an orderly attempt is made. You drive through the broken streets and the heart suddenly is lifted by a swatch of pastel-colored fronts, gleaming black iron railings, gas lamps on the stoops, brightly painted window frames. John Doar came to the Restoration Corporation in 1968 from the Justice Department. He had been in the Justice Department since 1958, arriving as an Eisenhower Republican from Wisconsin. In 1961, new Attorney General Robert Kennedy was afforded one look at John Doar's work. Bobby Kennedy's blue eyes flashed. "Isn't there some way that we can have his door locked so he can't leave us?" Kennedy said. "It wouldn't look terribly nice for me to be chasing after him down the street, would it?"

By the end of the summer of 1973, John Doar felt he had little more to give to Bedford-Stuyvesant. After nearly fifteen years of long hours and low public-service salaries he had college educations to worry about. He decided it was time to earn money and intended to leave before Christmas. That was before the phone call from Yale, and the one that followed some days later from Francis O'Brien.

"Would you like to come down one night and talk to the Chairman?" O'Brien said.

Doar said he would, and a date was made. Francis O'Brien had never met John Doar, but he knew him. John Doar is a legend to anybody who has worked the streets of this country and has had to work with the tensions and fears brought about by the divisions of race and class.

* * *

Doar came into the Rayburn Office building at seven at night. In the Judiciary room, Peter Rodino was conducting the hearing into Gerald Ford's nomination as Vice President. When O'Brien slipped up to Rodino and told him Doar was in the building, Rodino left the hearing.

"I have eight people I'm talking to," Rodino said.

"I understand," Doar said.

"Have you made up your mind on whether there should be an impeachment?" Rodino asked.

"I have not," Doar said.

Doar mentioned that he just did happen to have read *The Federalist Papers* before coming down to see Rodino. "The real important thing is the language of the articles of impeachment, if it ever comes to that," Doar said. He began to tell Rodino how careful wording had produced indictments of three law-enforcement people in Mississippi arising from the murders of three civil-rights workers, Andrew Goodman, Michael Schwerner, and James Chaney.

Doar sat in a chair alongside Rodino's desk. This tall, somber-faced, monotone-voiced man impressed

Rodino as he has impressed anybody else who ever has spent five minutes alone with him. There is in John Doar, under his silence and under his mixture of propriety and informality, a terribly fierce fifteen-round fighter. Peter Rodino, who grew up in a tenement in the First Ward of Newark, sensed this immediately. For all purposes, Rodino was risking everything he had or hoped to have upon his selection of a special counsel. If he was going to go down, Rodino kept telling himself, he at least wanted to go down with a strong guy.

At eight o'clock, Rodino went back to the Ford hearings. As Doar left the office, Francis O'Brien said to him, "If you take this job you're going to be hit. Are you prepared for public exposure?"

"Sure I am," Doar said. "I've been divorced, but that's no problem."

He went back to the Congressional Hotel and sat in the room and thought. In the morning he called O'Brien.

"Nothing I heard last night changes my mind about this job. This is no job you volunteer for. I won't lift a finger to get it. I'm not going to call you or anybody else. I'll wait to hear from you. If I do hear from you."

Doar went back to Brooklyn.

6

"The President talked with Mr. Haldeman."

* * *

In Washington one afternoon, Frank Thompson, Jr., a New Jersey Congressman who is Chairman of the House Administration subcommittee handling contingency funds, looked over a typed resolution that was about to be sent to the Government Printing Office. The resolution called for an appropriation of a million dollars to be given to the House Judiciary Committee. Thompson handed it to an assistant who then had it sent to the Printing Office. Later, with the House about to shut down, Majority Leader O'Neill took the floor to announce the business to be conducted on the next day. O'Neill read from a list which included such as H. Res. 8053, to establish within the Bureau of the Census a Voter Registration Administration for the purpose of administering a voter-registration program through the Postal Service. O'Neill finished and everybody went home for the night.

The next day, freshly printed copies of the House Administration subcommittee's resolutions were passed to members at the start of the day. There was a resolution calling for funds for the printing of the record of the proceedings unveiling the portrait of the late Philip J. Philbin; another resolution—H. Res. 605—was to authorize markers in Statuary Hall for the location of the desks of nine former Members of Congress who became President. And then there was H. Res. 702— which was "to authorize that the further expenses of the investigations and studies to be conducted pursuant to H. Res. 74 by the Committee on the Judiciary, acting as a whole or by subcommittee, not to exceed $1,500,000, including expenditures for the employment of investigators, attorneys and clerical, stenographic, and other assistants for the procurement of services of individual special consultants or organizations thereof."

The bureaucracy, in all its language and totally hidden meanings, was about to enter full motion against Richard Nixon.

"Tip, what do they need all that money for to go after an innocent man? Goddam, we can't be investigating the President," O'Neill remembers one Congressman saying.

"Well, you're not against the House looking into the situation, are you? Hey, you must be kidding. Nobody likes it. But we've got to show the public we're doing something or they'll be bullshit."

Wayne Hays, the Chairman of the Committee on House Administration, came to the front of the House to introduce the resolution. The clerk sitting behind him was ordered to read the bill. The clerk's flat dull tones went out into the chamber and became lost in the talking and laughing of the few members in the chamber.

During the reading, Hays called out, "Mr. Speaker, I ask unanimous consent that further reading of the resolution be dispensed with, and that it be printed in the *Record*."

Carl Albert called out, "Is there objection to the request of the gentleman from Ohio?"

No voice was raised.

John Wydler, a Republican, got up. "Mr. Speaker, I make the point of order that a quorum is not present."

Albert said, "Evidently, a quorum is not present."

O'Neill stood. "Mr. Speaker, I move a call of the House."

* * *

Each Congressman has a large electric clock in his office. On the rim of the clock there are twelve amber light bulbs. Now in each office, and in the dining rooms and committee hearing rooms, the clock gave three loud buzzes and three of the amber lights came on. Quorum call on the House floor. Members have fifteen minutes to get to the floor and be recorded present. There are many different combinations of lights and noises to summon Congressmen, from one buzzer and light to a civil-defense test warning of all the way up to twelve, which are rung at two-second intervals at eleven o'clock on the second Wednesday of each month. This time, the three bells brought 398 Congressmen to the floor. As they walked into the chamber, they inserted small plastic IBM identification cards into slots on the back of seats. Immediately, on a huge electronic scoreboard, over the press gallery, a dot appeared next to the name of the Congressman, showing he was present.

With a quorum present, the slowest dance began.

MR. WIGGINS: *Mr. Speaker, I have a parliamentary inquiry.*

THE SPEAKER: *Will the gentleman yield for a parliamentary inquiry?*

MR. HAYS: *I yield to the gentleman.*
MR. WIGGINS: *I thank the gentleman. Mr. Speaker,
was the committee amendment agreed to?*
THE SPEAKER: *It was not.*
MR. WIGGINS: *The issue under consideration is the
committee amendment?*
THE SPEAKER: *The gentleman is correct.*

On the floor, they walked about, slumped into seats,
leaned over, talked with the next one, got up, ambled
to the back, lit cigarettes and cigars, talked, laughed,
disappeared into the cloakrooms, came back, wandered up and down the aisles. The press gallery had
only two or three drones at work. Congress is rarely
covered by newspapers or television, and this most
certainly did not appear to be a day with any import
to it at all. The spectators' galleries were half-empty.
Sitting in one narrow section on the Republican side
were three White House people in charge of Congressional liaison. Dark suits, blond hair, cipher faces.
They watched, unconcerned. After all, this was just
some more dull, ceaseless, meaningless, dragging
House business.

David Dennis, the picture of a country lawyer from
Indiana, took the floor to fight for the White House.
"Is the gentleman aware of the fact that this Committee on the Judiciary already has an active impeachment investigation under way? That we have nineteen
people working full time on that subject? Is the gentleman aware that we have two hundred thousand dollars left in the account for this session, and that, in the
regular course of events, at the first of the year, we
will get at least another six hundred thousand dollars,
without getting a penny under this resolution?"

He was starting on the road he was certain was the
safest, supporting the President, and he never was to
leave it for a full year.

Dennis of Indiana, Dickinson of Alabama, Hays of
Ohio, Thompson of New Jersey stood on the floor and

bickered over the commas and periods of a resolution. Halfway through the debate, Hays announced, "Mr. Speaker, I yield five minutes to the gentleman from New Jersey, the Chairman of the Judiciary Committee, for the purposes of debate."

Rodino stood up. "Mr. Speaker, I regret sincerely that while our esteemed colleagues on the Republican side protest against partisanship, they have raised that very issue . . ."

Now Rodino got into the gut of the issue: ". . . I have treated the members of that Committee and especially the ranking Republican members with the utmost fairness, not because I just wanted to be fair but also because one must be fair, especially in this matter. The Committee on the Judiciary has presently a staff of twenty-six attorneys. Of them, nineteen were selected by the Democrats and seven by the Republicans. That is better than a one-fourth ratio. I have never rejected or refused a request on the part of the ranking Republican member, the gentleman from Michigan, Mr. Hutchinson. We hired mail clerks, seven or eight mail clerks, to open the mail on this alone. The five GAO investigators were not hired by the Committee investigation funds. We requested them from the GAO. We have one office manager that we hired in order to be able to supervise the personnel. . . ."

At the end, Dennis still was complaining about the Democrats controlling all that money, and besides, it was just too much to waste on this matter.

MR. O'NEILL: *Mr. Speaker, will the gentleman yield?*

MR. DENNIS: *I yield to our distinguished Majority Leader, the gentleman from Massachusetts.*

MR. O'NEILL: *I thank the gentleman for yielding. Mr. Speaker, if it were not for the scandalous action on the part of this Administration, it would not cost anything.*

The vote then was ordered. Throughout the offices, buzzers sounded and lights gleamed again and Congressmen walked down hallways, were in elevators, the subway from the office buildings to the Capitol was closed for use by anybody but Congressmen on their way to vote. On the floor, the cards went into the slots and the yellow lights on the big scoreboard over the press gallery showed how each man had voted. And on a wall on the Republican side, a small yellow scoreboard showed the tally as it rose. The final vote was 367 in favor, 51 against. The House Judiciary was to receive one million dollars for its bureaucratic life.

Congress immediately did what it always does best: recessed for the Thanksgiving holiday.

* * *

While everybody was at home for the holidays there was sent to Peter Rodino's office a single piece of white paper, stationery from the Speaker's office, upon which was typed the message that there was this day deposited in the office of the Clerk of the House the sum of one million dollars as per the resolution passed on the floor of the House. The piece of paper was thick and crackly. If you rubbed your thumbs across its surface, the paper produced a loud, satisfying sound. The edges of the paper, however, were firm and sharp. If you were to run a finger quickly down the edge of the sheet of paper, the finger would burn. A nick from a paper razor.

In the newspapers, only three paragraphs were devoted to the special appropriation of one million dollars for the Judiciary Committee. But everybody who had been in Congress for any length of time knew that the story was so much more important than that. The committee would spend most of the million dollars on paper; stacks and reams and tons of thick white paper, the edges burning, nicking and, in time, taking on the properties of tempered steel. The burns would become slashes; the nicks would become mortal wounds. In Washington, a million dollars' worth of paper will slash to pieces the life and career of any man who so much as brushes against its edges.

* * *

On the Monday after the recess, Tip O'Neill spent the morning hearing Confessions, as he calls it. Congressmen who had been home in their districts came onto the floor to tell him of unrest over the question of impeachment. "Tip, everybody asks me when are we going to do something? What am I supposed to tell them? Damn, but they all want to know about it."

O'Neill took a seat beside Rodino. He asked again about progress in hiring a special counsel. This irritated Rodino; he wanted to work at his own speed; it was his life which had to be put up. He had been asking people throughout the legal world about John Doar. So far, nearly everything had been positive. Still, Rodino wanted to take his time.

"It has to be before Christmas, we absolutely have to have the man by then," O'Neill said. Rodino exhaled in disgust. He wanted to be left alone.

On the 14th of December, Francis O'Brien decided on one of the surest ways to make something either happen or not happen. He called the Washington bureau of the New York *Daily News*. The next morning, in Brooklyn, John Doar saw his name in the morning *Daily News* story. The piece, out of Washington, said that Doar was one of eight people being considered for the job of special counsel to the House Judiciary Committee. Doar's phone began ringing. "Oh, that?" John told callers. "My name always makes any list that has eight or more names on it. Once they get below eight, my name doesn't appear any more." The calls also came to Washington. Favorable calls. Doar would be very good.

At this point, *The New York Times* discovered that John Doar was leaving his position at Bedford-Stuyvesant. Doar did not inform the *Times* of this; he is not a politician. But the story did originate in New York City. While Doar is no politician, he knows one hell of a lot of people who are. None of Doar's people ever will admit that he had a hand on the mirror, although when the *Times* story got around Washington, everybody took it as fact that Doar was leaving Brooklyn to become Peter Rodino's special counsel. Francis O'Brien said he could say nothing. All he really knew about it was that Chairman Rodino and Mr. Doar had spoken to each other. Blue smoke, thank you, good-by. It now was a matter of a day or so before Peter Rodino sat in his office and asked his secretary to place a call to John Michael Doar in Brooklyn.

* * *

So far in this account, when the mirrors and blue smoke have been properly worked, when they are being touched and handled by politicians with ability, by human beings of some substance and honor, the formula has not come close to failing.

And so John M. Doar came to Washington. Melvin Laird assured people in the White House that Doar was a fine choice. "He will not find anything if there is nothing to find," Laird said. "We couldn't ask for anything more."

Which was a proper determination, providing that Richard Nixon was more or less innocent, as Laird at the time believed. The one who knew differently, Nixon, said nothing. He should have. For John Doar believes in everything that Richard Nixon does not. And John Doar is a fearsome opponent.

In 1965, Doar was assigned by the Justice Department to be in over-all charge of the Reverend Martin Luther King's march from Selma to Montgomery. On the final day, a warm overcast afternoon, Doar walked slowly up Dexter Avenue in Montgomery, up the hill toward the State Capitol, where Governor George C. Wallace had the Confederate flag flying over the American flag. Behind Doar, minutes away, just starting into the main part of town, were Dr. King and the first ranks of his huge parade. Doar was walking alone to check the streeets. The sidewalks were lined with hesitant, curious whites. In the window of a second-floor beauty parlor, a woman sat under the hair dryer, two beauticians alongside, all craning to see the beginnings of the horror of black masses who came walking to bring down a way of life that was hundreds of years old. The woman under the dryer pointed to John Doar, who was walking in the middle of the street, eating an apple. She said something. The beauticians sneered.

"It's a beautiful day," John Doar was saying as he walked.

He did not notice the three white men standing on the sidewalk under the beauty-parlor window. They looked at John Doar and spit. They were Collie Leroy Wilkins, William Eaton, and Eugene Thomas, members of the Ku Klux Klan from Birmingham. That night, on the highway from Selma to Montgomery, their car pulled alongside a car driven by Mrs. Viola Liuzzo, a white woman from Detroit, who had been part of the march. Collie Leroy Wilkins leaned out the window and shot Mrs. Liuzzo in the head. The FBI investigated the case and arrested the three, turning them over to local authorities. In Washington, John Doar was told that the three had been on the sidewalk in front of the beauty parlor and he had walked past them. Doar's face showed nothing. Inside, it was different.

The murder trial of the three Klansmen was held in a second-floor courtroom of an old white courthouse in Haynesville. When the jurors were given the case to deliberate, they sat in a room that had two windows looking down on the side and rear of the courthouse. The jurors leaned out the open window. The local people stood on the grass and looked up and talked with the jurors. One man—"Just put down that ah'm the Presbyterian preacher, Haynesville, Alabama"—whittled a tree branch. He looked up at the jurors. "Now you boys do your duty," he said. Everybody giggled. One of the men on the grass called up. "Can't see why there's so much of a fuss. Ah done shot a big buck nigger myself once. Nobody said a damn word of it. She was out with niggers." The jury waited a day and came back to tell the judge they could not reach a verdict.

In Washington, John Doar began to have papers made out that would bring the three men in federal court in Montgomery on charges of violating Mrs. Liuzzo's civil rights. After the papers were filled out, Doar went home and packed a suitcase. He prosecuted the case himself in Montgomery. The federal judge on the bench was Frank Johnson. As Doar methodically laid out his case, his eyes smoldering, Judge Johnson began to stiffen. Johnson began to explain things to the jury, shaping them for what he was going to insist that they do: convict the three. The night the guilty verdict came in, Doar's taut face relaxed. The three Klansmen would be sent to maximum-security federal penitentiaries for years. Doar went to dinner at the Elite Restaurant on Dexter Avenue. The Elite always was George Wallace's hangout. George C. Wallace once was quoted as saying of John Doar, "Somebody should get a shotgun and blow Doar's head off." Do not miss.

* * *

Out of the months of irritation, arguments, pressure, and resistance between Tip O'Neill and Peter Rodino, politicians from local clubhouses, there came a John

Doar as the man who would sit and examine and sift the possibilities of Richard Nixon.

On December 20, 1973, John Doar walked into the barrooms of the second floor of the Congressional Hotel. The building had just been taken over by the House as a supplementary office building. Doar had been given the entire second floor. He would staff the rooms with 106 people. Guards were posted at the lobby elevator entrances, and at the elevator doors on the second floor. Doar chose one long large room for the library. The windows looked out over what had been the hotel parking lot. Prison bars were sunk into the window ledges. Thick wire grating was bolted on top of the bars. Special locks were put on the door, which was reinforced with steel. The room took on the feel of a penitentiary; there was no way in or out. Bolted to the top of the wall at one corner of the room there was what appeared to be a stereo loudspeaker. A box covered with black fabric. It was a motion detector. Once this room would be locked for the night, the motion detector automatically would go on. Any movement in the room, if the door came ajar even slightly, would activate alarms in the offices of the Capitol Police, the Washington Police, and the Federal Bureau of Investigation. By the time a prowler coming into the room took his second step, half of Washington would be surrounding the building. On the ceiling in the middle of the room was the silver nozzle of a smoke detector. A cigarette left in an ashtray would precipitate howling alarms throughout Washington. The room became a silo for the weapons that were to be stored there.

* * *

On a Saturday afternoon in that week, December 21, Larry Kieves of West Seventy-ninth Street, New York City, another former neighborhood task-force worker in the Lindsay administration, took a White House press release dealing with President Nixon's personal finances, and he sat down at a table in the library. He reached over and ripped open a cardboard box containing seven-ply index cards. The top card was yellow. Under the first sheet of carbon was a pink card. Next were four green cards and their carbons. The last card in the packet was a blue one. Kieves typed the subject on the cards. He placed a double asterisk at the end. At the bottom of the card the asterisks were explained: "**PF-1-IG." Go back to personal finances, number one, inquiry general file.

Kieves was starting on a manual information-retriever system which was to be used in place of computers. John Doar does not like, nor believe in the use of computers. He says they are useless in any matter involving security because anybody can punch a computer and find out what it knows. He also feels computers break down so continually as to be useless in this, the most important matter the nation ever had been in. A computer is marvelous for a bank. If the computer breaks down, interest computations can be done when the computer is fixed. Checks can pile up for a day. Checks even can be sent back by mistake. The only damage is embarrassment. But here in this wired, barred room on the second floor of an old hotel in Washington, what John Doar regarded as the future of the nation was going to be processed.

"I have two rules," Doar said. "The first is, I don't want anything done by machine that can be done by a human being. The second rule is, never delegate anything that you can do yourself."

Larry Kieves finished typing his seven-ply cards. He separated them, got up, and began to insert them into file drawers. They were the first of 500,000 index cards which would be filed in this room and which would become a cross-filing system with a level of precision that approached life. As Richard Nixon inhaled, somewhere in the file cabinets, seven cards would breathe with him.

The system had been devised when Doar was in charge of the Civil Rights Division of the Justice Department, during years when young lawyers in the department spent all their time legally ending barriers to registration and voting of blacks in Southern states, particularly Mississippi. Voters were being required to take a two-question exam, one question asking for a statement of the duties of a citizen, the second asking for an interpretation of a section of the Mississippi constitution. By cross-filing index cards of white and black voters, the lawyers were able to prove that if a black man and a white man gave exactly the same answers to the questions, the black man failed and the white man passed. In cases where the black man's answer was better, his exam was lost. The card system had also been put into use during investigations of the murders in Neshoba County, Mississippi, of Andrew Goodman, Michael Schwerner, and James Chaney, and they also were used in re-creating the movements of James Earl Ray, who pleaded guilty to killing Martin Luther King.

The system, then, was designed to protect the rights of black citizens, the same rights that Richard Nixon had been helping erode through his five years in office. And now this system, once used against old sheriffs in Philadelphia, Mississippi, was simply being turned around to face Pennsylvania Avenue. As Larry Kieves placed the first file cards in the first drawers, Richard Nixon never felt the first burning, the first nick on his finger.

*　*　*

For now, in December of 1973, the ultimate weapon of the bureaucracy, paper, was being used to end the career of Richard Nixon. Paper does not lose interest, nor does it get tired. Paper never goes away. With men, climates change, perceptions alter. What is on paper remains constant. The paper is in files, its carbon copies in other files. A subpoena. Thick, folded legal-bond paper. The prosecutor's office has a copy, the court clerk has two copies filed, the lawyer of the person receiving the subpoena has a copy. Destroy one copy and three remain. Destroy two copies and still two copies remain. Postpone the hearing, protest it on legal technicalities, tie it up in the courts. Become sick and apply for further postponements. Take months, take years, it does not matter at all. The paper does not go away. It is there and everything is on it and there always is somebody ready to pull the paper out of the file and cause it to be acted upon. Paper defied the law of bribery.

* * *

Into the second-floor offices of the Special Counsel of the Chairman of the House Judiciary Committee came thirty typists. Most of them had been picked because they were graduates of Catholic high schools. They were trained by nuns to believe in causes, and now they were to work on another cause, the greatest search for justice in the nation's history. Doar's notion was that their work on a cause would reflect their backgrounds. Jane Ricca, thirty-nine, of Our Lady Queen of Martyrs parish, Forest Hills, Queens, New York City, one day typed for twenty straight hours. Lawyers working on documents gave them to her, took them back for changes, handed the papers to her again, took them back for more changes. Six and seven times her work on one document had to be completely retyped. Jane Ricca never shook her head or sighed. She typed. Each day, the amount of paper rose. Cartons came from the Ervin committee. Barbara Campbell, a typist, came down the street from the Cannon Office Building, swaying from the huge stacks of Xerox paper she was carrying to Doar's offices. This was the first of the 1.5 million sheets of Xerox paper used to make up the notebooks of the members of the House Judiciary Committee. The files grew, the library room began to resemble a newspaper city room, with desks jammed together to form one long desk, and paper piled all over the desktops. The architect for the Capitol had to be brought in. Workmen reinforced the library floor to accommodate the weight of all this paper. Two-drawer file cabinets became six-drawer file cabinets. And everywere, on every typewriter, on every carbon, on every card and paper in every file drawer, there were notations such as, "AP-26 A." This particular one had to do with White House media relations. But it really had to do with Richard Nixon, as did every other card and piece of paper on the second floor of the Congressional Hotel. Nixon could fly to San Clemente. He could have his lawyers protest and delay. He could ignore what was going on. He could rail and sulk. He could fly to Moscow, to Tel Aviv, to Cairo. There would be sun and service—the President does not make a phone call by himself—and the days would become weeks and the weeks would become months. The public would tire of Watergate, the newspapers would begin to write of other things. The President would say it was over: let us go on to something else. And always the paper mounted and the files grew thicker and higher and the typists typed. The paper grew, the edges becoming sharper, sharper, sharper. Soon Richard Nixon would feel the pain as the paper began to cut his life away.

* * *

Among the bales of paper received from the Ervin Watergate committee were many copies of Richard Nixon's daily diary. The copies had been surrendered peacefully by the White House. They were strange documents, detailing Richard Nixon's day to the minute. Doar read them himself, as did nearly all of the staff. There was something basically so twisted in a man who would detail his whereabouts this precisely that the effect of reading it was stunning. A typical account would be the day in Richard Nixon's life, shown on pages 116–117, Thursday, July 6, 1972, at what was called the Western White House at San Clemente.

The gossip in people drew them to the amount of time Nixon spent with his wife. From 2:50 to 2:51, he spoke to his wife. At 4:48 he met Mrs. Nixon at the pool area. By 5:02 he was returning to the San Clemente Compound residence. At 5:47 he went with her to the oceanside patio. By 6:19 he was back at the residence. This pattern repeated itself throughout all the diary pages. Through the days and nights of his life his diaries showed he spent a half hour, at the most up to an hour, a day with his wife.

Doar was more interested in the obvious implications. That Nixon would chronicle each movement of his life so thoroughly—all that was left out was his bathroom habits—meant that the man was so obsessed with the notion of his greatness that he wanted it recorded forever. The diaries were to be the basis for Nixon's New Testament.

The diary pages were piled up on desks in the typing rooms. As the diary pages were copied onto sevenply cards, the people were too busy to notice that when the overhead light came onto the pages, the edges of the daily diary paper glistened more than any other paper in the room. The finely ground steel—whitened by sharpening—of a terrible swift sword.

John Doar began to show lawyers on the staff a method used in the old days at the Justice Department. Doar took all the cards for a particular day out of the files, spread them on a desk, and began to examine them and move them around into different positions. "Sometimes you get to moving them around and you find the cards are telling you a story you didn't know," Doar said.

One lawyer, Bob Owen, was more than familiar

with the card game. He had spent twelve years with Doar in the Justice Department and he had been through everything. In Brownsville, Tennessee, someone walked into a meeting at a black church and asked to see Owen outside. As Owen came outside, five men with shotguns stepped out of the woods. Owen stared at them. "Put those guns down, I'm a federal official," Owen said. Confused, the men did not shoot him as they were supposed to. Owen walked back into the meeting.

In Neshoba County, Mississippi, a man reached into the car and put a .38 to Owen's head. Owen again said he was a federal official. "If you can't prove it, you're a dead man," the guy with the gun said. Owen slowly went through his pockets and came out with the card. The gun came away from his head.

When John Doar called him in January of 1974, Owen was in private practice in the firm of Patterson, Belknap & Webb, in Rockefeller Center, in New York. He made an arrangement with his firm which allowed him to take some time off to work with Doar in Washington. Owen also spent his weekends working with Doar.

Doar had made two major decisions about how the case should be conducted. He decided not to do any investigating of his own, but to simply pick up the materials gathered by the Ervin committee and the Special Prosecutor's office and work from there. He thought that an investigation, interrogating witnesses—on television—would give the public the idea that everybody was doing the same thing over and over and the entire idea of impeachment might lose its effect. Doar also decided to try to place Richard Nixon in the heart of the cover-up conspiracy, from the very day after the Watergate break-in occurred. The Watergate Special Prosecutor's office seemed to be concentrating on Nixon's activities from March 21, 1973, the day John Dean informed him of the "cancer growing on the Presidency." All of Nixon's defenses were based

PRESIDENT RICHARD NIXON'S DAILY DIARY
(See Travel Record for Travel Activity)

PLACE DAY BEGAN				DATE (Mo., Day, Yr.) JULY 6, 1972
THE WESTERN WHITE HOUSE SAN CLEMENTE, CALIFORNIA				TIME DAY 8:20 a.m. THURSDAY

TIME		PHONE P=Placed R=Received		ACTIVITY
In	Out	Lo	LD	
8:20				The President had breakfast.
8:21	8:23			The President motored by golf cart from the San Clemente Compound residence to his office.
8:28	8:33		P	The President talked long distance with Acting Director of the FBI L. Patrick Gray III in Washington, D.C.
8:40	8:41	P		The President talked with his Press Secretary, Ronald L. Ziegler.
				The President met with:
8:41	9:08			John D. Ehrlichman, Assistant
8:58	8:59			Alexander P. Butterfield, Deputy Assistant
9:10	9:15			The President met with his Personal Secretary, Rose Mary Woods.
				The President met with:
9:15	10:08			Henry A. Kissinger, Assistant
9:25	10:08			Sir Robert Thompson, author
9:25	10:08			Maj. Gen. Alexander M. Haig, Jr., Deputy Assistant
10:10	10:11			The President met with Mr. Butterfield.
				The President met with:
10:11	12:05			Mr. Ehrlichman
10:18	10:22			Mr. Kissinger
10:40	12:06			H. R. Haldeman, Assistant
10:40	12:06			Clark MacGregor, Campaign Director for the Committee for the Reelection of the President
10:40	12:05			Frederic V. Malek, Assistant Campaign Director for the Committee for the Reelection of the President
10:44	11:01			William E. Timmons, Assistant
11:00	11:01			Mr. Ziegler
12:06	12:08			The President met with:
				Mr. MacGregor
				Mrs. Clark MacGregor
				Ollie P. Atkins, White House Photographer
12:08				The Presidential party went to the lawn behind the President's office.
12:08	12:11			The Presidential party held a photo opportunity.
12:11				The President returned to his office with Mr. and Mrs. MacGregor.
12:11	12:12			The President met with Mr. and Mrs. MacGregor.

PRESIDENT RICHARD NIXON'S DAILY DIARY
(See Travel Record for Travel Activity)

PLACE DAY BEGAN				DATE (Mo., Day, Yr.) JULY 6, 1972
THE WESTERN WHITE HOUSE SAN CLEMENTE, CALIFORNIA				TIME 12:13 p.m. DAY THURSDAY

TIME		PHONE P = Placed R = Received		ACTIVITY
In	Out	Lo	LD	
12:13	12:14			The President met with: Mr. Butterfield
12:13	12:25			Miss Woods
12:26	12:30			The President met with: Miss Woods
12:26	12:32			Mr. Butterfield
12:30	12:31			Miss Woods
12:31	12:34			Miss Woods
12:37	3:00			The President met with: Mr. Haldeman
12:39	2:36			Mr. Ehrlichman
1:33	1:39			Mr. Ziegler
1:37	2:23			Miss Woods
2:50	2:51	P		The President talked with the First Lady.
3:03	3:05			The President motored by golf cart from his office to the San Clemente Compound residence.
1	3:24			The President motored from the San Clemente Compound residence to Red Beach with his valet, Manolo Sanchez.
3:26	3:31	R		The President talked with Mr. Ehrlichman.
4:26	4:46			The President motored from Red Beach to the San Clemente Compound residence with Mr. Sanchez.
4:48				The President and the First Lady went to the pool area.
5:02				The President returned to the San Clemente Compound residence.
5:24		P		The President telephoned Mr. Haldeman. The call was not completed.
5:28	5:29	P		The President talked with Miss Woods.
5:30	5:43		P	The President talked long distance with his Special Counsel, Charles W. Colson, in Washington, D.C.
5:47				The President and the First Lady went to the oceanside patio.
6:19				The President returned to the San Clemente Compound residence.
8	7:04		P	The President talked long distance with Secretary of Defense Melvin R. Laird in Washington, D.C.
7:10		P		The President telephoned Mr. Kissinger. The call was not completed.
7:15				The President and the First Lady had dinner.
10:23	10:25	P		The President talked with Mr. Haldeman.

on the belief that the March 21 conversation with
Dean was when the fight had to be made. And it was
regarded in the White House as a fight that could be
won. But over in the Congressional Hotel, John Doar
was starting his attack from another direction. He was
patrolling the streets of a year earlier, starting with
June 18, 1972. When Doar first began working with
his own staff, in January of 1974, one of his staff people, Evan Davis, who is confined to a wheelchair, told
Doar, "From what we've got already, I think the one
tape I want to hear, if I had to hear any tape, is for
June twenty-third."

As Bob Owen began on the project, he went
through stacks of reports for that period. He took the
cards for June 17 out and spread them on the table.
Owen was looking for some great flash to come to him.
It had happened once before, during the investigation
of the murders of Goodman, Schwerner, and Chaney.
One of the suspects was named Cecil Price. When
Owen spread the cards out onto the table one day he
began to re-create Cecil Price's day. As he moved the
cards, Owen suddenly realized that Price could not
have been able to drive five miles and catch up with
a car in the amount of time he said it had taken
him. Owen called the FBI and had them go onto the
road in Philadelphia, Mississippi, and do exactly what
Price had claimed to have done. The agents reported
back that Price had to drive at a hundred and fifty-
five to cover the ground he claimed. And Price's
twelve-year-old car couldn't do any more than eighty-
five.

Now, as Owen looked down at the cards for
June 17, then June 18, he was hoping that some place
along the line he would see something. He worked in
the crowded library room, smoking True cigarettes and
drinking coffee out of a paper cup in a plastic holder.
He has less sandy hair now than when he went up
against shotguns in the 1960s. He has the deep lines
in his face and the roll in his voice of an Albany,

Texas, dirt farm. Owen knows it spoils everything when people find out he went from Albany on scholarships to Choate and then Princeton. Therefore, at times his speech—"Well now, you just ain't goin' to hardly make it that-a-way"—is used as a disguise.

"McCord," Owen said as he looked at the cards. "McCord is fired from his job at the Re-Election Committee. Fine. But now where is Liddy on the eighteenth?"

"He is still listed as working for the committee," Maureen Barden said to him.

"When did he leave the committee then?" Owen asked.

"Not till the twenty-eighth. He refused to talk to the FBI and they fired him."

"Not till the twenty-eighth? And only when they had to get rid of him?"

"I'll get it for you," she said. People like Maureen Barden working in the library were so obsessed with the subject matter that they sometimes used the files only to verify oral answers. As Bob Owen got into the work, he, too, could feel the heroin effect of the stacks of paper in the room.

Maureen Barden's records showed, of course, exactly what she had told Owen.

Owen decided that the White House was trying from the start to contain the investigation. McCord was fired right away. The entire re-election group, and the White House, knew the Watergate break-in was a G. Gordon Liddy operation. Yet they never fired Liddy until nine days later, when they absolutely had to. Doar was right. Nixon had to be in on it from the start.

Owen began to work on the files and cards. Haldeman. Ehrlichman. Dean. Mitchell. And Nixon. Immediately after the 1972 election, Owen's eighty-six-year-old father wrote him a letter. One sentence of the letter stuck with Owen forever: "Richard Nixon is the most dangerous man in the history of the world."

Typewriters clicked. Drawers were pulled in and out. Winter rain lashed the parking lot under the library room windows. The noises and movements in the room would be the same when the first spring sunlight appeared. Everything moved slowly and there was no way to stop it.

—— 7 ——

"The night-school students are saving the country."

* * *

The hand that rocked the bureaucracy into motion was found, of a Saturday night in June 1974, wrapped around a glass.

"Will you drink a Manhattan?" Tip O'Neill asked a man joining the party.

The man thought about it.

"I asked you, will you drink a Manhattan?"

The man thought more about it. Agitation showed in O'Neill's face.

"The reason I'm asking you if you take a Manhattan is that there's no bar here and it takes them too long to bring us back a drink. So I ordered two Manhattans for myself and you can have one of them if you want."

This was in the early part of the evening, when more than forty people came into the private dining room of the Wayside Inn, at Chatham, on Cape Cod, the people gathering there in celebration and admiration of the thirty-third wedding anniversary of Tip and Milly O'Neill and simultaneously the sixtieth birthday of Milly O'Neill, that number being loudly announced to all by her husband.

O'Neill was standing in a circle of people, everybody talking. O'Neill talking back to everybody, when his son Tom—who was running, successfully it turned out, for Lieutenant Governor of Massachusetts—placed a hand on his father's elbow. "Dad, I just want to tell you this one thing."

O'Neill, looking straight ahead, the eyes taking in the entire room—politics is for backcourt men—said out of the corner of his mouth to his son, "Hey, I can listen to five conversations at once. Just keep telling me what you want me to know."

His father went back to the group. "Chuck, is the weather really that bad? I thought Bantry was part of Cork. Cork's not supposed to be that bad. Oh, it's in West Cork? Oh, they have bright spells. That's good. Bright spells. Dick, old pal, you look good. Mary, darling! How are you? What will you have to drink, dear? Are you playing any golf, Paul? Well, I played today. You know what happened the other day out there? I'm on the third hole and there's a ball on the fairway and I don't know where the hell it came from. And here coming through the woods from the other fairway is Jim St. Clair. I said to him, 'Hey, Jim, what are you doing over here?' He just gave me this shrug and I kept on going my way. Stop to talk to him? Oh, I wouldn't do that. It just so happens that we're both members of Eastward Ho. Do I know him? I'll tell you a story about Jim St. Clair. One day a long time ago I got a call on a Sunday morning from a man whose son was arrested for drunken driving the night before. The boy was a senior at West Point. He was taking a summer course at MIT. The boy had been out and he'd had a few and the officer arrested him in Central

Square for drunk driving. Well, I get a call from the father. He said the son'll be thrown out of West Point. Could I help? Well, geez, a kid goes to his last year in the Academy. I'm not going to let him get into trouble over a few drinks. Of course, I'll try to help. I told him I'd get my brother Bill, who was alive then. Practicing law, you know. Well, Bill calls the guy and the father says there's ten thousand in it if you could get my son off. My brother says, no, one thousand will be the charge, and I *cahn't* guarantee you anything but a pretty good try. The father said, no, it has to be ten thousand. My brother Bill says, no, I'll charge you a thousand. So on a Sunday morning we all come to court. I take a seat and the clerk comes up to me and says the judge wants to see me in the back. So I go back there and the judge says, 'Tip, what are you doing in here?' So I tell him the story of this West Point lad. When I finish I go outside and by now the father and the boy are in court. And with them is Jim St. Clair. During the night, it seems the father had gotten nervous after he arranged to have my brother Bill. And the father asked for the name of the biggest lawyer in Boston and they told him Jim St. Clair. So Jim St. Clair sees Bill and I starting to leave and he says to the father, 'You know, I'm not as experienced in a city court like this one. I think you're better off with Bill O'Neill here.' So the father said all right, and Jim St. Clair went off to play golf and my brother handled the case. Well, it was in Cambridge, and you got to know Cambridge. The policeman got up on the stand and my brother asked him, 'Did you know that this boy was a senior at West Point and that he is taking summer courses at MIT in order to better prepare himself to defend his country, and that he just pulled off to the side of the road on Saturday night to sleep off the exhaustion?' And the cop said, 'No, I didn't. If I had known it, I never would have allowed the court clerk to issue the summons.' Now you see, in Cambridge at the time the cop did not issue the summons.

The court clerk did. So now the cop decided not to press the matter any more. At the same time he himself didn't have to rip up any ticket or anything. It was up to the court clerk to revoke the summons. Which of course he did and the case was over. And now I'm going to show you where Jim St. Clair is so smart. Remember the father telling my brother Bill about ten thousand dollars for the case? Well, he gave Bill three hundred dollars on the first day. Now for the rest of the bill, seven hundred, it was pulling teeth to get it out of him. Anyway, Paul, old pal, you look marvelous. Hey, what about all this food? Come on now, let's eat." He began steering people toward the buffet table.

At the end of the night, on his way to the car, O'Neill led his wife into the crowded smoky taproom of the Wayside Inn. He waited until George McCue, who plays the piano, finished a song. Then he came through the tables and up onto the small bandstand. He wanted to do one thing before the evening was over.

"My name is Tip O'Neill and I fool around in politics. I just want to sing a song for my wife, Milly, on her thirty-third wedding anniversary. I want to sing the song they played on the day we were married. The name of the song is 'Apple Blossom Time.'"

George McCue began to play the song on the piano and O'Neill's barbershop voice boomed out the start of the song.

> *I'll be with you in apple blossom time,*
> *I'll be with you*
> *To change your name to mine. . . .*

He sang through the smoke to his wife, selling her a love song in front of the strangers. You thought automatically of Nixon and his Haldeman and Ehrlichman, standing in the doorway of the amber light of the room, smirking and starting to leave, secure in the

119

absolute belief that no such open, old-fashioned people could be dangerous. If O'Neill was Congress's idea of a leader, how could they be hurt? How could a man who sings to his wife in public ever qualify as an opponent? At the last note, O'Neill broke into a neighborhood cheer, his voice coming up from the sandlots:

"Milly Miller O'Neill! Yeah!"

* * *

The next day he went to Washington, taking with him in all his mannerisms and speech the loud, crowded life of the streets and of the frame houses of Cambridge and Boston, and the life as a politician that is much a part of the area. There is no way to understand what went on in Washington in the summer of 1974 unless you realize that what happened was because of politicians. Ask Peter Rodino what was the single most important thing he had to do to bring about the impeachment vote against Richard Nixon and watch the Constitutional scholars pack around to hear his answer:

"When I was able to hold Mann, Thornton, and Flowers, then I knew it could be done," Rodino tells you. "I had to have them. Once I had them I could start to put it together."

Put it together. A vote. The basics of clubhouse politics. He had to know that he had the votes of James Mann of South Carolina, Walter Flowers of Alabama, and Ray Thornton of Arkansas. With these Southerners for impeachment, the needed Republican votes would not be impossible to obtain. Let the scholars debate the narrow versus broad interpretations of the Constitution as the most meaningful thing to come out of the impeachment. Peter Rodino knew it was the votes that did it. The politics, not the scholarship of the matter.

And, from his position, Tip O'Neill knew it was the job of causing the bureaucracy to move that enabled everything else to happen. He knew this because he was a professional politician, and you might as well know a little bit of what these people are and where they come from.

* * *

For a little island, it has caused so much pain. In 1845, there was a great potato famine in Ireland, people in remote areas trying to subsist on yellow winter grass and, finally, crazed, entering the black torture of cannibalism. Everywhere in the country there were children unable to close their mouths, the lack of calcium in their bones preventing their jaws from working. Three O'Neills—Pat, John, and Mike—left Cork City for the terrible ocean crossing to Boston, and the promise of jobs with the New England Brick Company. In Boston, the first money the brothers gathered that was not needed for food went directly into the Irish stock market—cemetery plots. The next money Pat O'Neill had—in 1855—was spent going home to Ireland and bringing back a wife to America. A son from this marriage was Thomas P. O'Neill, Sr. He was raised to be a bricklayer. In 1900, he won a seat on the Cambridge City Council. On the day his son was born—Thomas P. O'Neill, Jr.—the father was picketing Harvard with people from the bricklayers' union. The only thing better a man from Cambridge could say about his father is that the father was elected President on the day he was born. For Harvard, until it began to grow up in the last fifteen years, always regarded the people outside its gates as leaves upon the streets.

In 1914, Thomas P. O'Neill, Sr., received the highest mark in a Civil Service test for the job of superintendent of sewers and sanitation for Cambridge. There were 1700 men on the payroll, none of them Civil Service, which meant that O'Neill was in charge of hiring and firing. His hand immediately reached out to touch more jobs. He married the executives of the Edison Cambridge Gaslight Company, a joining together worth hundreds of jobs to O'Neill, Sr. In North Cambridge, he became known as "The Governor." He ran the North Cambridge Knights of Columbus baseball team, was President of St. John's Holy Name Society and—strict Irish rather than dreaming Irish—head of the St. Matthew's Temperance Society. Nobody in his house was allowed to wear anything that did not have a union label on it. No clothes were ever thrown out—there always was a society for the needy. And all the children in the household were brought up to regard the first Tuesday after the first Monday in November as the most important day of the year. When Tip O'Neill was fifteen, he was out ringing doorbells to pull people out of their houses to vote for Al Smith for President and Charley Cavanaugh for Massachusetts State Representative. Tip O'Neill, in charge of half a precinct, reported at the end of the day that only four people in his area did not vote, and they were out of town.

Tip O'Neill hung out with a large crowd of kids at a place called Barry's Corner, and without anybody mentioning the fact, O'Neill was the leader. One of them, Red Fitzgerald, remembers his mother saying that Tip O'Neill was going to be a bishop. "He never pulled a dirty trick in his life, so how could he miss?" Red says. O'Neill always had a way to keep the crowd around him, and also to be useful to them. He had a job as a night watchman at a brickyard, and he fixed up the outdoor telephone pay station with a nail into the contact so that his nightly crowd of visitors had free phone service. It was in the middle of the Depression and nobody had the nickel for a call.

By 1931, O'Neill was out of high school and earning $21 a week as a truck driver for a brick company. November of that year was cold and work was slow. O'Neill took courses at Boston College High School at night, then entered Boston College. Neither the college nor the O'Neill family publicizes his scholastic achievements, although Boston College prints his picture on its literature and considers him as perhaps the school's most important alumnus. Meanwhile, if Boston College ever were to falter, Harvard would be more than happy to claim O'Neill as its own. The matter of academic brillance was brought up over the summer in Washington, when Peter Rodino (who never went to college) and John Sirica (scholastic background at best vague) were busy showing the nation that honesty might be important.

"The night-school students are saving the country," Mary McGrory, the writer, was saying one day. "I don't think Sirica or Rodino spent a day in a regular undergraduate school. And I'm certain that Tip did not."

"Oh, no, he went to Boston College," she was told.

"Oh, yes, but thank God it wasn't serious," Mary McGrory said.

In his education O'Neill did himself and the country a favor by not following the traditional path of entering law school before going on to politics. During the early months of 1973, a Tip O'Neill, attorney at law, trained in the deviousness and tiny facts of the law, never would have come walking into Carl Albert's office saying that Richard Nixon was going to be impeached. That was too outrageous, and also too true, for a lawyer. Tip O'Neill, attorney, would have had instilled in him by professors the knowledge that he had not a scintilla of evidence upon which to base any judgment at all of Richard Nixon's status in February of 1973. O'Neill, not being a lawyer, did not know that he was using such terribly unsure methods as instinct, a little anger, and a boxcar full of common sense.

The fact that O'Neill is not a lawyer gives singularity to his success. It always has been extremely difficult for legitimate people to get into politics because the base of the American political system has been built on the needs of lawyers. They come out of offices that are one flight over a drugstore and have gold lettering on the windows that says "Attorney at Law," and they come into the political system because time and occupation make it the place to be. Lawyers are not lashed to a normal person's work schedule. Always, a lawyer can switch his schedule around so he may attend a City Council meeting at one-thirty on Thursday afternoon. Also, as the nation grew and started to sprawl at the turn of the century, the lawyers then in command drew up codes so intricate, so tangled that no citizen could ever do business with a government agency of any size, from town to federal, without the service of a lawyer. Particularly a lawyer involved in politics. Many of the rules and regulations adopted throughout the country, most still in effect today, carried with them the unwritten admonishment, "Bring Extra Money!" This, in envelopes, for sliding under the table. Corruption to benefit lawyers was built into the government structure as if it were notarized. Today in politics, at a place where most men must start, it seems to be almost solely a place for lawyers. Judges appoint referees, lawyers, for mock-auctions of foreclosed properties. The judges appoint lawyers known in the business, and politics is the business of judges. The items spiral upward to a point where you have foreclosure proceedings on multimillion-dollar mortgages and the judge appoints a referee, a monitor, again a clubhouse lawyer who receives as high as $30,000 on a million-dollar matter; receives the $30,000 for doing approximately nothing. How much of this does the lawyer keep for himself and how much does he hand back to the judge? That depends upon the bargaining ability of both. If they were to strike a poor deal, a quarrelsome deal, somebody might hear of it and a district attorney would consider the subject a prime opportunity for career advancement. Other matters between lawyer and judge can be settled in ways that almost can be traced; the judge has a son and daughter who attend expensive colleges, all bills paid from a sort of scholarship set up by a lawyer.

Because there is money to be made from the system, lawyers get into politics as a business necessity. The reasoning is that lawyers are necessary in government because government makes and deals with laws, and lawyers are best equipped for this. But laws are things to be understood and obeyed by everybody, so why should the making of laws be left to a small inbred system? The major reason for the presence of so many lawyers in government is, of course, the economics. Less than 5 per cent of the lawyers in the nation ever stand on their feet in a courtroom. That is too unsure a life. A public payroll, however, is very sure. Representing a contractor who does business with government agencies—where the lawyer knows people through his political life—also can be considered a certainty. And then the financial structure of public life makes office-holding a dream for a lawyer. Most local and state and many federal elective posts allow a person to practice law on the side. Senator Jacob Javits has a law firm on Park Avenue in New York City. State Representative Michael LoPresti has a law practice in Boston. The rewards produced by the situation cannot be counted. Therefore, at the start of a career, it bothers not a politician to have to live in the state capital for four or five months a year, at a salary of perhaps less than $15,000, because his law office in his home district is producing a living for him. But for a college teacher with ideas, or a steamfitter with ideas, it is financially impossible to serve in a state legislature. Some think or dream or even try. Always the result is the arithmetic of family bills makes politics impossible.

Left mainly to lawyers, then, the pursuit among most politicians on a local level is for the great prize: a judgeship. Judges receive excellent money, serve lengthy terms, and have short working hours and long vacations. In New York, higher courts pay up to

$49,000 for terms of fourteen years. Foraging rights appear to be limitless. The scramble for a judicial vacancy becomes so intense that the entire political structure of a county can be frozen while councilmen and assemblymen and leaders push and swirl and bargain —often openly passing money about—for the judgeship.

Tip O'Neill represents the ones who came another way. If you see the system work on a local basis, you wonder how anybody worth while ever lasts through it and gets anyplace. But for O'Neill, there was no way he could not be a lifetime politician. Clearly, the viral containers in his genes held, who knows, a couple of thousand years of the ability to control, to calm others, to decide without being abrasive, to be affable while the insides boil. For good politicians, real politicians, are not created in law school or in bank vaults. They are born, as their fathers were born, and the father of the father before them, and then back through the ages, with this viral container of public life in the genes. Just as the ability to play a piano in concert or to write a lasting novel is present at birth.

As a senior at Boston College he ran for Cambridge City Council. His father did virtually nothing to help him, and he lost the election by a hundred and fifty votes. The arithmetic still is fresh. "I got four thousand votes," he says quickly, "and thirteen hundred of them were from North Cambridge. I should have gotten eighteen hundred votes there. That's if I pulled what I should have in wards seven, eight, nine, ten and eleven. What happened? My father said to me at the end of the election, 'You know, you never asked me for help.' The woman across the street said the same thing to me on election day. Her name was Mrs. Elizabeth O'Brien. She was an elocution teacher. She called over to me in the morning, 'Good luck, Thomas. I'm going to vote for you even though you didn't ask me.' I told her I'd known her all my life. 'Mrs. O'Brien, I used to run to the store for you. I didn't think I had to ask you.' And she said to me, 'Tom, people always like to be asked.' Well, you could of punched me right in the nose and I wouldn't of felt it."

The next time he ran he was working in a small insurance brokerage and real-estate office in Harvard Square. The insurance business can serve the same purpose as a law degree to a politician, but he never did very much with it. In the election this time, there was a candidate named Tierney who had to be beaten for a seat in the State Legislature. A few days before the election, an old pro named Foley said to O'Neill, "You've done well for a beginner. I don't want you to feel bad when you lose." O'Neill began to come continually late to street-corner rallies. He was too busy working the side streets and asking housewives to vote for him.

On election night, Tierney took a hotel room, had a few drinks, then slept for an hour. He showered and changed his clothes in order to look fresh and vibrant when acknowledging the cheers later on. Tierney came to his headquarters and, whistling softly, asked to see the results from his prime area, Ward 11, Precinct 3. Eleven-three contained St. John's School, its rectory and convent. Tip O'Neill had worked the area so thoroughly he owned it. The slip of paper for 11-3 was handed to Tierney. Tierney's soft whistle stopped, as did his heart. The results from 11-3 showed O'Neill with 712 votes and Tierney with 163. Rested, showered, Tierney went out in search of a pulmotor. And in his own headquarters, a rumpled, sweaty, flushed Tip O'Neill let out the first of what were to become a lifetime of election-night laughs.

Some years later, 11-3 was given a thorough campaigning by Congressional candidate John F. Kennedy. The area is changing now, with college students moving into houses that have been cut into small apartments; but if you walk into the kitchen of a house where lifelong residents live, the woman will point to a chair at the kitchen table and tell you, "He came in here and he sat right there. God rest his soul."

One day after the 1962 Congressional elections, Jack Kennedy saw O'Neill in the White House, and he said, "Say, Tip, how did you do in eleven-three?"

"You know, only thirty-four people voted against me," O'Neill said.

"And I'm sure you have the names and addresses of every one of them," Kennedy said.

In 1935 O'Neill was almost twenty-three when he won this first election. Also in that election, up in another section of Cambridge called Greasy Village, Leo Edward Diehl, twenty-two, won a seat in the legislature. He won as much by his powers of observation as anything else. One morning, at the start of the campaign, Leo was out in the streets in time to see one Father John Geoghegan driving a woman named Peggy Dolan in the general direction of Peggy Dolan's job in Boston. You would have had to cut off Leo Diehl's head to make him forget this.

Some mornings later, Leo Diehl was on the same street at the same time and here was Father Geoghegan again driving Peggy Dolan to work. Leo grunted.

It then happened that in the core of the campaign, Leo Diehl heard that Father Geoghegan was going door to door on behalf of Leo's opponent, a man named Hillis. When this news was brought to Leo Diehl, the candidate showed no outrage. He simply asked for somebody to give him a lift. As the car pulled away, everybody on the sidewalk was surprised at the calmness with which Leo received the news, very bad news for his campaign because in Cambridge a priest's word had power second only to money.

The friend driving Leo Diehl said to him, "Where are we going?"

"I want to drop by and say hello to Peggy Dolan."

Peggy Dolan was shocked by Leo Diehl's accusations. "I do not go out with Father Geoghegan! I just let him drive me to work.

"Besides," she said, "Father Geoghegan goes steady with Theresa MacNamara."

Theresa MacNamara was a local dance instructress who had danced the parish to death. Leo immediately had his friend drive over to Theresa MacNamara's dance studio.

"We do not!" Theresa MacNamara squalled. "All we do is the Texas Tommy together."

Leo Diehl persisted. Soon, in tears, Theresa Mac-Namara said:

"He calls me Pussy Cat."

Later that night, grunting, grimacing, Leo Diehl pulled himself up the rectory steps and rang the doorbell. When Father Geoghegan appeared, Leo Diehl said, "I just wanted your permission for Theresa Mac-Namara to come around with me tonight and tell all the people that she's your best girl and that she wants them all to vote for me."

Father Geoghegan started to faint. He pulled himself together long enough to agree that he would make the rounds on behalf of Leo Diehl himself.

"Make sure you do," Leo said. "By the way, I don't know what's the matter with you. I'd rather jump on top of Peggy Dolan than Theresa MacNamara any day."

In January of 1936, O'Neill and Diehl entered the State House for the first time. It was the beginning of a relationship which is closer today than it ever was. And it also was the true beginning of a political career for Tip O'Neill.

There is in this country no place that could even be suggested as being anywhere near the Massachusetts State House for bone politics. Throughout the nation, the complaint with state legislatures is that they are part-time bodies. Not even that in many places. New York, supposedly so efficient, has a state legislature which meets in January and averages three days a week until the late spring. After which it is regarded as a criminal offense for the legislature not to be recessed well in advance of the closing days of the school year, thus giving legislators time to open summer houses, pack their kids' clothes for camp, and plan vacation trips. In Massachusetts, the legislators prefer to sit forever. They usually have to be driven out of the building, practically at gunpoint. If a Massachusetts legislator is removed from his game, his sport, his very life, then all that is left for him to do is return home to his wife and family, and in Massachusetts anybody can have a family but the true goal of life is to be a politician; or, true term, a Pol. It is not uncommon for the Massachusetts Pols to sit in the State House throughout the summer, arguing, spreading rumors, using the phones, and—true glory—plotting against each other.

But in this they are so right. For who would leave a building, and what possible reason could he give, where the life in its halls is dedicated to the memory of the actions of such as former Governor—among other things—James Michael Curley? Ask anybody in Boston about Curley and they will grope for a place to begin; there is so much to tell. Well, in 1933 new President Franklin D. Roosevelt offered Curley the post of United States Ambassador to Poland. From the State House there came a great cry, "He'll pave the Polish Corridor." And from James Michael Curley himself, in a face-to-face meeting with Roosevelt, there came, "If Poland is such a great place, why don't you resign and go there yourself?"

8

"I hear you play tennis."

At the start of the summer, Richard Nixon sat at his
desk in his Oval Office with the political people, Anne
Armstrong, Dean Burch, and William Timmons,
seated across from him.

"How's Goldwater?" Nixon asked.

"He seems fine, but you know, Mr. President, I
couldn't control one minute of his life," Burch said.
Burch, from Arizona, had been one of Goldwater's
chief campaign aides in 1968.

Nixon said, "Oh, the President knows that you
couldn't do anything like that with Goldwater."

Nixon then said, "How's it look on the Judiciary?"

"Well, Railsback is on the fence."

"Railsback. Well, there's time."

"Smith is okay."

"Fine."

"Flowers is all right."

"We're heating him," Burch said. "We're talking to

people at home. Newspaper editors. Radio and television."

"Sure. The people at home are behind the President," Nixon said.

"Mann," Burch said.

"Heat him up, too. All of his people support the President. Loyalty. They're loyal to the President."

The matter always was discussed in the abstract, Nixon referring to himself only in the third person. There were times during the years of Watergate that the thing grabbed him inside and threw everything around: when Haldeman and Ehrlichman had to resign on April 30, 1973, Nixon became an aimless drifter, flying everywhere, doing nothing. People in the White House say he was unable to function and the country had no true leader. But then there were times such as this meeting, when he sat in his office, discussing everything in the abstract, certain that he never had done anything wrong.

"He was the President," Dean Burch says, "and the President never does anything wrong because he is the President."

None of the political people talking to him—before leaving to defend him—ever had asked Nixon about the facts of the Watergate case. One simply does not go up to a President of the United States and say, "What about this? Are you guilty?" It has been our system up to this point. Most human beings who reach the White House, in any capacity, immediately become so royalty-prone that there appears to be no way for the situation to change.

After the meeting, Burch and Timmons sat down to discuss their defenses in the House and Senate. Timmons was a Congressional liaison man, a White House lobbyist on Capitol Hill. Burch was much stronger. He is listed as a Conservative from Arizona, but he is much broader and smarter than the connotations of any label. As an FCC Commissioner, he became known as the most independent of the commission. He kept saying that he saw no reason why in this country a newspaper should be allowed to own a television station. This belief—big communications is as dangerous as big government and big labor—brought choking sounds from the throats of the nation's finest liberal and conservative newspaper publishers who also owned television stations.

Burch and Timmons talked about their problems with a defense based on executive privilege regarding the President's tapes.

"I see something like this as only a last resort," Burch said. "I'd rather just let everything come out. It won't be all that bad. Now the whole thing is March twenty-first. All right, there's some things in there not so good. But on balance, you can come out of that all right. It's just a strong circumstantial evidence. No, we're all right on that March twenty-first. So I just don't see why we keep stonewalling it on the rest of the tapes. Let them out."

"It's about the end of the line for talking about executive privilege," Timmons said.

"We'll wind up sounding as bad as O'Neill," Burch said. "Save me from any more of this 'The future of the nation' that he keeps telling everybody. He's just playing plain old hardball politics."

* * *

Tip O'Neill made the fight out of his lair, the Democratic cloakroom of the House. Two double-hinged doors on the Democratic side of the chamber, doors with dull stained-glass windows, lead into the cloakroom. It is a long, narrow windowless room with a curved railroad-car ceiling. Brown leather couches and armchairs are set against the wall, linen handtowels covering the tops of the chairs. Brass ash stands are alongside the chairs and couches. The far end of the room is kept in darkness; somebody is always stretched out for a nap.

As you come into the room from the floor, there is a sink and an aluminum lunch counter. Lemon-meringue pies sit on racks inside tall circular plastic containers. The only thing missing from the scene is a couple of flies buzzing the meringue pies. The lunch counter is run, of course, by a black. His name is Raymond and he is quick to say, "I don't know nothin', I don't see nothin', I don't hear nothin'." In a cabinet on the wall there is a first-aid kit and a Life-O-Gen oxygen inhalator. The carpeting, wine with yellow and black speckles in it, is worn in spots. There should be much more dust in the carpet to emphasize the age from which its pattern is derived. The thought immediately occurs to you as you walk into the cloakroom that Congress is afternoon baseball.

The only thing to contradict this is a switchboard in an alcove, and fourteen phone booths. A red wall-phone next to the page boy who runs the switchboard is the one used to contact O'Neill.

He came into this room in June with a new weapon, another mirror, a forty-page notebook put together by William Hamilton and Staff, pollsters, for William Welsh of the American Federation of State, County, and Municipal Employees. The topic sentence of the report said, "In April our study shows 43 per cent will vote for a Congressman who is inclined to vote for impeachment; 29 per cent would vote for a Congressman who would not be so inclined and 28 per cent feel the Congressman's stand on impeachment would make no difference at this time."

A further interpretation of the figures showed that "50 per cent of Republican voters will vote against a Congressman who is inclined not to vote for impeachment, while only 7 per cent of the Democrats will vote for a Congressman who is inclined to vote against impeachment."

Into the cloakroom at this point came Dan Rostenkowski of Illinois. Cook County, Illinois. Rostenkowski is six-foot-two and he weighs about two hundred and twenty pounds. Dan Rostenkowski always says to people, "Do you know what is black and blue all over and is found floating in the river?"

"What?"

"A person who tells Polish jokes."

Rostenkowski had an opinion on impeachment. This was formed when he heard a number of fine, compassionate liberals demanding that Richard Nixon be both impeached and then thrown in jail for income-tax evasion. Rostenkowski did not like impeachment so much to begin with. When he heard income taxes mentioned, he nearly put his hand through the table. Income taxes! One sixth of Chicago would have to go to jail if they started a push on income taxes. In Chicago, the form always has been that the politicians receive huge, scolding headlines when they are caught stealing and selling high-rise sites and parking-lot locations, all in cash, all unreported. The public reads the headlines and then, joyously, gives the politicians in question the largest votes ever recorded. And that ends it. The other word the liberals were using—jail—is such a bad word in Chicago that Rostenkowski could not even get himself to mention it. He simply gave off a feeling of cold death and let it go at that.

O'Neill went right to Rostenkowski, because Rostenkowski is Mayor Daley's play-caller with the Illinois Democrats in Congress. A word from Danny is a word from the Hall. Deviation? Try Russia, not Cook County.

"Danny, old pal, did you see this poll yet?" Tip O'Neill said.

"What poll?" Rostenkowski grumbled. He despises polls, but he had to ask about a poll because he is in politics and he is supposed to ask about a poll.

"It shows here that we could pick up as many as eighty seats the way it's going now," O'Neill said.

"Whew."

"And it shows here that there is no way for a Congressman in an urban district to win an election against anybody if he doesn't vote for impeachment."

"Where does it show that?"

"Here, look. Only seven per cent of the Democrats will vote for a Congressman who is against impeachment. That means a Republican could beat a Democrat in a city if the Republican is for impeachment and the Democrat is against it. Can you imagine that? Say, that's right. You represent a city, don't you, Danny?"

O'Neill began to show the poll around. He told Thaddeus Dulski, who comes from upstate Erie County in New York, that the poll showed all rural votes being lost to a Congressman who is against impeachment. "But you don't have any farms in your district," he told Dulski. Dulski grumbled. He had a religious belief in the Presidency. He also had a lot of farmers in his district. Out on the House floor, when O'Neill saw Angelo Roncallo, a Long Island Republican, he said, "Hey, Angie, old pal. Geez, but you really love it down here, don't you? Angie, I want you to know something. My door is always open to you, as you know. And to show you how much I think of you, Angie, my door is still going to be open to you next year when you're not going to be in the Congress because of this impeachment." O'Neill gave a great, fun laugh. Roncallo laughed with him but not as much.

It was like the first round of a fight. He jabbed, stepping in with the jab, and found the other guy went back right away. Then he bent down and tried a left hook to the body. The guy was right there for him. He always had said that the other guy was going to get knocked out. Now, after the first couple of punches, he was certain of it. There would come a time in this fight, probably on a hot afternoon sometime after the middle of August, with everybody out on the floor, and he would load up, hook off a jab, and Richard Nixon would go home in a blanket. No question. As far as O'Neill was concerned, the fight was off the boards.

* * *

At lunch one day in the House dining room he showed me why there was no other way.

"Here, look at the door and then you'll know as much as I do," he said.

In the doorway, looking around for a table was Congressman Joseph Moakley. Moakley was swinging his arms, clapping his hands in front of him, beaming and laughing, a hand reaching out to slap somebody on the shoulder.

"He just learned he has no opponent in the primary. Louise Day Hicks decided that she didn't want a primary. Now look at the other guy behind him."

The other guy was Congressman James Burke. He was motionless. He is an old Irish fox who keeps everything behind a straight face. But this time, a bleakness, a physical pain, was set in his face.

"He's got an opponent," Tip said. "Some young guy from the Milton City Council filed to run against him in the primary. There is no bad news like that news."

Moakley came past the table. Shaking hands, slapping shoulders.

"You must feel pretty good, old pal," Tip said.

"Thank God and anybody else who had anything to do with it," Moakley said.

Burke came by. "Hello, Tip," he said quietly.

"James, you look disturbed."

"Not at all, I'm fine."

"What are you going to be doing this weekend?" Tip asked him.

"I've got to go home. I've got a couple of parades I've got to go to."

"When was the last time you went home for a parade?" Tip said.

"Oh, I don't know."

"It doesn't matter because this year you'll be carrying the flag for the whole time," Tip said.

He laughed and Burke did not.

When Burke was gone, O'Neill said, "You see what an opponent can do to you? I think Jim can win all right. But the money kills you. Cost you a hundred thousand dollars. Now if an opponent you can beat is this disturbing, imagine what it's like to face one that you might not be able to beat. Imagine what it must be like for some of these Republicans. You're facing an election in November and the only issue in the country is how you stand on impeaching the President?"

* * *

There were two occurrences at the beginning of July, occurrences which had been taking shape for many weeks. When they arose, they added to the tension of the situation. One was more revealing of the enemy than it was dangerous. The second appeared, for a brief moment, a direct threat to the success of the impeachment process of the House.

The first occurrence, the one that revealed, began its life on June 4, 1974, when Jeb Stuart Magruder came up the dirt hill to the steps of the administration building at Allenwood Prison camp in the dull, working hills of central Pennsylvania. Loitering by the front door were two inept thieves from Brooklyn, their presence dictated by their performance with stolen treasury notes.

"It could get hot here this summer," one of them, Mr. J. G., said to Jeb Stuart Magruder. It was the first time J. G. ever had spoken to a man from Washington who was not part of the FBI.

"And it gets good and fuckin' cold in the winter," the second thief said to Jeb Stuart Magruder. Thus he, too, spoke for the first time in his life to somebody from Washington.

Magruder mumbled something and then looking around, in a first-day daze, he said, "Neil Gallagher here?" Magruder walked on without waiting for an answer. He knew what he was looking for. Out in the world, at the end, Jeb Stuart Magruder was confessing and repenting in a book and in newspaper interviews. He even went so far as to get his wife on television to dispense wisdom and gather sympathy.

Neil Gallagher—former Congressman Cornelius E. Gallagher of Bayonne, New Jersey—had in December of 1972 pleaded guilty to charges of income-tax evasion and had been sentenced to two years. On June 16, 1973, he appeared at the Federal Courthouse in Newark and turned himself in for the start of his sentence. Gallagher was slapped into handcuffs, leg irons and chains, and taken through a fence of cameramen to the Federal House of Detention on West Street in Manhattan. Two weeks later, he was shipped to Allenwood, a group of four dull brick buildings sitting in the businesslike hills of central Pennsylvania. Allenwood is supposed to be a country club as prisons go. There are no walls or guard towers. Fifteen miles away, Lewisburg Penitentiary rises out of the corn fields, a terrible rust-brick and iron smokestack of a place. All of which is a matter of degrees. A jail is a jail, and at eight o'clock of a night at Allenwood, with the mind becoming a scrambled egg, what does it matter whether or not the place has a wall and guard towers? Petty regulations in a minimum-security institution are so numerous and unnerving that many prisoners prefer the places with walls and guard towers because rules are less intricate.

At the end of six months in Allenwood, Gallagher applied for community visits with his wife and family and was turned down. Egil Krogh of the Watergate case came to Allenwood, was in the place for three months, and then was allowed off the grounds with his wife for twelve hours. Gallagher then had a disbarment hearing in New Jersey. A court order was delivered to Allenwood calling for Gallagher to be furloughed for purposes of the hearing. Usually a minimum-security prisoner is furloughed for purposes of a hearing such as this. The authorities suddenly decided that Gallagher would be shipped in handcuffs and chains. When the Federal Bureau of Prisons in Washington was asked about this, their answer was that Gallagher never had applied for a furlough for the disbarment hearing.

At a parole hearing, a caseworker for the parole board looked at Gallagher's applications and said they were fine, but there were some areas where it was plain to the parole people that he was not cooperating.

"Where?" Gallagher said.

"Well, we know you took a beating on your supposed association with Joseph Zigarelli. But, ah, Mr. Rodino, for instance, certainly has an awful lot to hide and you probably could show us the way to get at it. So far we have received no help from you."

It became plain to Gallagher that he was going to do the maximum time on his sentence. This is so rare for a person in Gallagher's circumstances—nonviolent crime—as to be remarkable. Gallagher began to concentrate on his physical condition, running three miles a day. He worked in the prison office as a typist— "I'm training to be a Kelly girl," he wrote friends—he was elected head of the inmate grievance committee. However, the days would not let his mind rest. Agitation began to cause the skin on his cheeks to tremble.

Gallagher had been in Allenwood for a couple of weeks short of a year, and he knew he was facing at least another six months, on the day that Jeb Stuart Magruder came up the steps looking for him. At dinnertime on his first day as a prisoner, Magruder came up to Gallagher. "I hear you play tennis," he said. The inmates had cut a tennis court out of the dirt of the camp grounds; Gallagher was one of those who played on it.

The first time Gallagher went on the tennis court with Magruder, it was plain Magruder was not interested in tennis. He stopped the game and went off to the side of the court and spoke to Gallagher.

"If you could do anything to help, the President really would be able to do something for you," Magruder said.

"Like what?" Gallagher said.

He remembers Magruder saying to him, "Peter Rodino is going to be wiped out. We've got plenty on him. If you could help, that's all we need. When we come up with something on Rodino, the public will be so revolted that the President could make it through. And then you, you'd be out of here clean. With a pardon. You could practice law."

Gallagher said nothing to him. At this time, he had received notice that his home in Bayonne had been foreclosed, and the court was going to issue an eviction notice. He was worried about his younger children having to leave house and school, the only security they had in these times. And the idea of six more months in Allenwood gnawed at Gallagher. One day in prison is an awfully long time. Magruder, whose right hand is full of bribes, drew visions of success again for Gallagher.

Some days later, Magruder had a visitor. He said it was his lawyer. The two sat on the rough cement patio outside the prison's crowded indoor visiting room. Gallagher, working in the office, saw the two of them talking. Afterward, Magruder told him the lawyer had said they were just about to ruin Rodino.

"He'll be here again, and if we have anything for him, he can go right back to Bill Timmons," Magruder said.

Neil Gallagher went to the office and placed his name on the list requesting permission to use the phone. There is one pay phone in Allenwood. It takes about three hours to gain permission to use it, and then an inmate must stand on line waiting his turn.

Neil Gallagher called Congressman John Murphy in Washington. It now was almost the end of June 1974, and the House Judiciary was deep into the closed presentation of evidence.

John Murphy let O'Neill know about it. O'Neill went directly to Peter Rodino.

"Peter, there is an awful lot going on. There is nothing that can come out of the woodwork on us, is there?"

Peter Rodino shook his head violently. "Absolutely nothing."

O'Neill nodded and the conversation was over.

"That's all you had to say to him?" O'Neill was asked later.

"Yes."

"He didn't want to hear more about it?"

"No. He hated what he heard."

"And the answer was all it took to end the whole thing?"

"Yes. We had to believe each other. He knew what we were into as well as I did."

People in Rodino's office had heard that Nixon people were around Newark asking questions about him. And they also heard that in Washington Patrick Buchanan of the White House staff was trying to sell the line to reporters about Rodino being connected. In the minds of so many of the people in the White House, starting with Nixon and going naturally to the Buchanans and on down, all Italians were out of the fraudulent movie, *The Godfather*.

There also was much talk about immigration bills— all immigration bills go through the House Judiciary— which would show that hoods were being brought into the country. The last thing a criminal from a foreign country wants is his name on anything: a passport, visa, official document of any type. As for gaining admittance to the country, there are perhaps two hundred places on the border of New York and Canada where a person can drive a car back and forth and see nobody in charge of anything. In the small world of the defendants and accomplices inside the White House, these things were not known. Because, after all, there had to be something, someplace. Nobody ever would think of an Italian like Rodino gaining greatness.

Nobody knew how they thought better than Peter Rodino himself. When the tapes subpoenaed from Nixon began to arrive at John Doar's offices on the second floor of the Congressional Hotel, Rodino and Edward Hutchinson, the senior Republican on the committee, sat and listened through headphones. One day Rodino listened as the voice of Richard Nixon, speaking to John Ehrlichman, said:

"The Italians. We mustn't forget the Italians. Must do something for them. The, ah, we forget them. They're not, we ah, they're not like us. Difference is, the . . . they smell different, they look different, act different. After all, you can't blame them. Oh, no. Can't do that. They've never had the things we've had."

"That's right," Ehrlichman said.

Nixon's voice dropped. "Of course, the trouble is . . ." Now his voice went even lower. "The trouble is, you can't find one that's honest."

A great sadness came over Peter Rodino. He made sure Hutchinson heard it. Then he asked Hutchinson if Hutchinson would agree to leave out this part of the tapes for hearing by the full committee and, perhaps someday, the public. Rodino knew it would inflame Italians who had voted almost to a man for Nixon, and thus materially damage any support Nixon had left. But Rodino simply wanted the remark to go away. Hutchinson said he would do what Rodino wanted. Rodino said thank you, and the remarks about Italians did not get beyond the room. They did tend to remain, however, in Peter Rodino's heart.

There was one afternoon when Rodino was sitting for a television interview and, while the cameramen were changing film, Rodino was talking about what it was like to be an Italian-American and in his position.

"You know, all these things that have been written, all these movies, things like *The Godfather,* and they have concentrated so much on this business like . . . the Mafia. And here we see . . ." Rodino held his hand out as if he were supporting something. His eyes gleamed. "And here we see Sirica and Rodino upholding the institutions of the country. I just can't tell you the pride I feel in being an Italian-American. And I know how John Sirica feels about it, too."

Vernon Hixson, one of the television men, said, "That's beautiful. Now when we start the cameras this time, try to say it exactly the same way."

The cameras came on and Rodino was asked a question about his Italian heritage. A glaze of formality came over his eyes. Two expressive hands clasped into schoolroom propriety.

"I am naturally proud of being an Italo-American," Rodino said. "But we must remember that the heritages of all the people of the world are in our Constitution and it is our duty to uphold the Constitution regardless of what our individual backgrounds are."

"Stop for a minute," Vernon Hixson said to the cameramen. Then Hixson said to Rodino, "Congressman, that was very nice. But would you please say exactly what you said before, the thing about being abused by people using this word Mafia."

Rodino's chin went from side to side, slowly. He said in a near-whisper, "That wouldn't be appropriate."

"Oh, but you said it beautifully."

Rodino went into himself a little bit more, leaving behind a little smile. "No," he whispered, "I couldn't say a thing like that. Not when I'm dealing with the Constitution."

The second occurrence, the dangerous one, first began to take form months before. It grew out of the nature of the political business. On one hand there was John Doar, un-elected, with working methods that were as strict and severe as they were successful. Security is a rather simple word to Doar: it means you say nothing to anybody. As politicians essentially are elected washerwomen, information often their only visible means of support, this secrecy made some members nervous. "We're so damn secretive that we're going to impeach Nixon in secret and he'll never know it," William L. (Bill) Hungate of Missouri complained. There also was impatience with Doar on the part of Jack Brooks of Texas, Jerome Waldie of California, Joshua Eilberg of Pennsylvania, and Robert Drinan of Massachusetts. And underneath this, the problem of Jerome Zeifman, who had been bypassed for the special counsel role in favor of Doar.

Zeifman began saying that Doar's presentation was stripped of all human ingredients. He said Doar had taken the case apart like some gigantic erector set, left it on the table completely disassembled, and never commented on how it should be connected. Doar and Francis O'Brien, Rodino's administrative assistant, regarded Zeifman as a destructive element, and the complicated matter of keeping thirty-eight human beings in some sort of harmony became even more trying.

During the long hours that Doar sat in the Committee, purposely dull, daring never to go near the advocate's role, David Dennis of Indiana—briefed, primed, prepared by James St. Clair and totally committed to Nixon's defense—hammered away at Doar. Let's get to March 21, 1973, Dennis was saying. Prove to me what the President did wrong. You've got a lot of circumstantial evidence here. Where is your proof, where is your proof, where is your proof? Dennis, too, did not notice it when Doar, in the midst of a dreary afternoon, poked through the material regarding Nixon, Haldeman, and Ehrlichman on June 23, 1972. Later, it was to cost Dennis his seat in Congress—he was defeated in the 1974 election. But at this point, with the first heat of a Washington summer making the days longer and more dragging, Dennis's continual table-thumping was effective.

At which point Zeifman and William Dixon, a counsel working for him, took their own course inside the committee. Dixon, working with Waldie, Eilberg, and Drinan, prepared a series of twelve memos which he felt would put some fire into the presentation. The memos pointed out the differences between the edited tape transcripts released by the White House, and the flat material read by Doar. One Dixon memo concentrated on Dennis's and St. Clair's defense of Nixon's conversation with John Dean on March 21. Dixon's memo said the conversation showed clearly that Nixon had told Dean that they had to buy time making a $120,000 payment of hush money to H. Howard Hunt. The memo circulated in the second week of June. By the 14th of June it had been leaked to the newspapers. Zeifman and Jack Brooks, meanwhile, were pushing to have Richard Cates, another staff counsel, present information to the Committee. Cates would have the fire they thought they needed.

The result was problems inside the Committee, and a major problem on the outside when the leaks appeared in print. The White House jumped on the leaked memos as an attempt by anti-Nixon people on the Committee to destroy the President. A number of voices quickly were raised in agreement. Newspaper columns—particularly Joseph Kraft in *The Washington Post*—began saying that the process had gone too long, that it was in danger of losing all momentum. A cartoon showed the impeachment ship sinking.

One evening Doar met Congressman Wayne Hays at the elevators in the Congressional Hotel. Hays had an office for his House Administration Committee on the sixth floor of the building.

"You blew it," Hays said to Doar. "You're never

going to get the votes now. You had 'em and you lost them. You've taken too much time."

The conversation was more than a passing one to Doar. Hays headed the committee that provided the funds for the impeachment staff.

The talk, of course, came to the House. "I don't know, they tell me that Doar is an archivist, not a prosecutor," O'Neill said one morning. "I don't know what to say. I know it's taking too much time. Everything is timing, and these delays are starting to get me worried. They've got that Johnny Rhodes working for them here and, believe me, he is about the best you'll ever see."

* * *

On June 25, a Monday—Monday is the day party leaders such as O'Neill set aside for hearing "Confessions"—O'Neill began to hear complaints from too many about the slowness of the hearings. J. William Stanton of Ohio said, "We need action one way or the other. Can't you get it off our backs? Instead of the impeachment being an asset to us, now it's starting to hurt us. I heard it everywhere over the weekend. They're not only disgusted with Nixon, they're disgusted with me, too. They don't think anything is happening."

"It was the same from everywhere," O'Neill recalls. " 'Tell us where we are; tell us where we're going to be,' that's all I was hearing."

He sat down next to Peter Rodino and began leaning on him.

"Will you get off my back?" Rodino said.

"Hey, I have two hundred and forty guys on my back," O'Neill said.

O'Neill wanted a definite schedule set for the hearings, the vote in Committee, the start of debate on the House floor. Rodino, who had been spending long hours in seclusion, poring over the rafts of paper, did not see how he could set a date. He reminded O'Neill again that O'Neill was not a lawyer, that he did not understand. O'Neill pressed for a date to be set. Rodino resented it. But at the end of the long, tortuous day, at one o'clock in the morning, Rodino sat in his office with John Doar and Francis O'Brien and told them that they had to set a schedule for the rest of their work.

O'Brien and Doar were against it. They wanted nothing to interfere with what they felt was a satisfactory pace.

"You don't understand, the leadership is on me," Rodino said.

"What leadership?" O'Brien asked.

"Well, Tippy is on me and they're on him and we've got to do it."

"What does Tippy O'Neill got to do with it?" O'Brien asked.

"You don't understand, it's the leadership," Rodino said.

"Wait a minute," O'Brien said. "Tell me one thing. What has Tippy O'Neill got to do with you? You're a committee chairman. Tell me where he can start telling you what to do."

"You don't understand," Rodino said.

"No, Francis has raised something," Doar said. "What right has O'Neill got interfering with your business?"

Rodino looked up at the ceiling and thought. As he thought, the blue smoke and mirrors disappeared. All that was left was the pages of a rule book. He, Peter W. Rodino of New Jersey, was Chairman of the House Judiciary Committee, and as such, under law, he was in charge of hearings into the possible impeachment of a President. As for Thomas P. O'Neill, Jr., of Massachusetts, he was the Majority Leader of the House. There is not one thing in law or House Rules that says the Majority Leader has the right to do anything.

Rodino's head came down and his hand hit the desk. "You're right! He has no business bothering me at all, and I'm going to tell it to him tomorrow."

In reconstructing the late-night conversation, both O'Brien and Doar are proud of the manner in which Rodino took on the matter. Doar adds, "And that was the night we set the date. We said we'd be ready for Committee debate on July fifteenth and we'd have a vote by July twenty-seventh. And we kept pretty close to that schedule, didn't we?"

Apparently, after Rodino brought his head down and slapped the desk, he not only summoned his anger, but he summoned a full complement of mirrors and blue smoke back into the room.

For, the next day, along with an angry rebuke to O'Neill, Rodino also gave him a timetable for the impeachment. O'Neill had the dates typed in his office and shown around the floor. The effect was sharp. Again, the moment you particularized the matter of impeachment, showed anything on paper, there was an immediate tightening of people. The more you made impeachment a reality, the more people were inclined to accept it.

With the schedule set, O'Neill went to dinner that night at Duke Zeibert's Restaurant. He told a table full of people, "I got on Peter's back and he resents it. He should. When the rest of us are all forgotten, Peter is the guy who is going to be in history. Remember what I tell you."

In the Committee, Rodino's hand also came down. Zeifman and Dixon were rebuffed. The danger passed, and the momentum of the paper, which never had slowed, again became apparent. The staff would compile, before it was to finish, forty-two books of information. The normal Xerox paper had a tendency to stick together and there was so much copying to be done that separating the paper was a major job in itself. They switched from Xerox paper to expensive bond paper in order to speed the process. The workload became so heavy that one night, at two in the morning, girls coming to a Xerox machine in the Rayburn Building, found Peter Rodino, in shirtsleeves, running the machine himself.

9

"Now, let me tell you what is going to happen."

* * *

Bob Owen was coming down from New York on a Thursday now, and staying in the library until Monday morning. He would sleep a half-hour a day on a couch in Doar's office. In the early evening he would walk up to Pennsylvania Avenue, have a couple of martinis and a steak, and then return to the office and work through the night and through the next day. Coffee and cigarettes—he was onto three packs a day —took care of the rest of him. Owen would read the cards and other evidence pulled out of the files during the day. Then at night, after dinner, he would dictate his notes, which were to form parts of the "Statement of Information" book being worked on. Owen worked on thirteen of the first thirty-eight volumes put out by the group.

Owen was scheduled to go on vacation in July from

his law firm. He couldn't wait. This would give him the chance to work full time in the second-floor library.

* * *

Up the street, in the Capitol building, Tip O'Neill began to think of gathering votes. He told the newspapers he was keeping no lists. Which was true. He was not keeping lists on paper. He was keeping them in his head.

When Congressman Teno Roncalio of Wyoming asked O'Neill to come out and speak at a dinner in Cheyenne, O'Neill said absolutely yes. Roncalio's district voted over 75 per cent for Richard Nixon in 1972 and now that Roncalio was going to be voting to impeach Nixon, any and all help he could get would be appreciated. O'Neill and Roncalio flew out of National Airport in Washington at eight o'clock in the morning, landed in Wyoming in mid-afternoon. On the way from the airport to the motel, the driver took O'Neill on a tour of Fort Custer. Great cottonwoods and Austrian pines, trees that can take the Wyoming winters, lined the roadway.

"Pershing lived in that house," the driver said, pointing to a brick house set back on lawns.

"Geez, it's beautiful," Tip said.

"Here's the parade ground," the driver said.

"Geez, what a parade ground!"

"Smell the air," the driver said.

Tip sniffed the light, sparkling early summer air.

"Geez, it's terrific. Say, where do you run the rodeo?"

"Oh, it's right across the way there."

"Do they make any money?"

"I guess so."

"Much Indian fighting out here?"

"Sandhill massacre was near here."

"Where was Custer massacred?"

"That was three hundred miles north of here.

"See the tepees over there," the driver said.

"Look at the Indians!" O'Neill said. "You mean they're actually living there?"

"Yessir."

"Wow!"

"You enjoy it out here?" the driver said.

"Well just look at it," Tip said.

Blue mountains sat against a blue sky with moving white clouds, the mountains appearing very close in the clear air, but they were actually twenty-five miles away.

"Geez, beautiful," Tip said. "What a place."

He pulled on his cigar and looked out the window.

"I could last about a day out here," he said.

At the motel, I was standing at the bar having a drink when the pilot of the plane, on his way to his room for a nap, stopped by to say hello. He had a Coke.

"Well, what do you think about Nixon getting impeached?" he said.

"Oh, I wouldn't know. I just flew out here with Congressman O'Neill. I wouldn't dare ask what he thought, I wouldn't do that."

"That's funny," the pilot said. "Just before we were getting off the plane I asked him and he told me that Nixon was going to get his ass thrown out."

The dinner drew a crowd of 500 people, the backbone of influence in Cheyenne. Roncalio told the audience that it was the first time a Majority Leader of the House was ever in Wyoming. He made that sound important. Roncalio then said, "He is one of the two or three men in whose hands rest the impeachment process in the House of Representatives."

O'Neill went right to his William Hamilton and Staff poll. The numbers had grown somewhat during the flight from Washington.

"In the 1948 election, ninety-two per cent of the Democrats voted for Democrats, and ninety-two per cent of the Republicans voted for Republicans," he said. "But now there is a thirty-nine-per-cent break-away from the Republican party because of the impeachment matter. And the poll shows that eighty-five per cent of the breakaway will vote Democratic."

That set the audience up. He went into economy and inflation for a moment. Then he stopped and put on black-frame glasses and arranged paper on the lectern in front of him.

"And now we come to the important topic of the hour, and probably in the entire history of the country. Impeachment. I try not to speak off the cuff on this matter. I use prepared notes for this."

You could feel the tension run through the room. Ranchers who had flown in for the meeting, big, long-armed Westerners, put the coffee cups down without causing the slightest clinking sound. Bankers held their cigarettes near the ashtrays and leaned forward. The woman seated next to me held her breath. It was the first time any audience in Wyoming had heard impeachment discussed by anybody involved in it. Now it wasn't a story in the newspapers anymore. And now on the dais O'Neill was not a likable story-teller any more. He became erect, careful. A major leader of government. His face was set and his voice did not come soft and easy. In slow, measured terms he began by saying:

"Justice Brandeis said, 'Decency, security, and liberty alike depend on the system in which no man is above the law. This mandate is a daily thing, answerable at all time on all matters.'"

Heads nodded every place in the room. O'Neill carefully scanned the room from left to right. He gave side glances at the dais. There, too, heads nodded in agreement.

You've got to be kidding, O'Neill told himself. *Nixon doesn't have a vote in the room. If he doesn't have a vote here, how the hell can he hope to get one from anywhere.*

". . . base men will drive out honorable men."

Again, the heads nodded.

"Now, let me tell you what is going to happen."

The feeling was the same as being in a courtroom waiting for a jury verdict.

"I doubt if forty Congressmen have openly said what they'll do. I, of course, never have said anything. Now when the witnesses are finished in the Judiciary, there will be three days to review the case. There will be a markup of the bill. On the twenty-sixth of July, the Judiciary Committee will have voted on the bill and reported to the full House. On August fifth, the bill will go to the Rules Committee. There then will be two weeks of full debate on the floor of the House or a hundred hours of debate, whichever comes first. The Republicans feel sixty hours will be sufficient. The vote in the House will come on August twenty-third. If the Judiciary Committee votes to impeach the President, then the President will be impeached by seventy-five votes in the House. If the President does not obey the Supreme Court order to turn over the tapes, the number will be much greater. In my opinion, if the House of Representatives votes to impeach by the seventy-five votes or more, then the Senate will convict the President in a trial, if there is one.

"We are not happy. But we are strong in our hour of sadness. Our country is strong enough to survive. Jerry Ford will give this nation the stability it needs."

He reached down and brought up a big ten-gallon hat he had been presented with earlier. He put it on.

"The rest of the nation isn't wise to Wyoming, and I won't tell them what you've got here," he said.

They laughed, got up, and applauded. Three quarters of the room had voted for Nixon, but there was not a mumble or a disgusted look.

Later, as the plane flew back through the night to Washington, Teno Roncalio tried to sleep, and O'Neill sat in the darkness and smoked a cigar and looked out the window. He said it just once.

"Wyoming," he said. "He doesn't have a vote in Wyoming. This thing has been over for months."

*　*　*

July. Bob Owen had not been to bed for three days. His teeth were stinging from cigarettes. He was up to four packs of True cigarettes a day. It now was the 15th of July and the House Judiciary Committee was coming to the end of its closed hearings. The full committee meeting, the debate and vote on impeachment, was now scheduled to start on the 20th. John Doar was driving to complete his final summary of information. This was the book that was to change his role. It was not a statement. He could not read it as a neutral. It would be his summation, his position on the matter. He would come out for the first time as an advocate. He would sum up his facts, give his interpretations, and he would take on James St. Clair's defense theories. Take on St. Clair and take on Nixon.

Owen worked with the cards of June 17, 18, 19, 20, 1972. They were filed by time, subject matter, and people—asterisks for cross-references everywhere. As Owen put the cards out, moving them, matching them, he could see a pattern of arrangements for a meeting on June 20th. Phone conversations, gained from logs and long-distance toll tickets, showed John Dean being called on the 18th and brought back from a trip to the Far East. The group in California—Mitchell, Mardian, Magruder, LaRue—came back from California. Attorney General Richard Kleindienst, in Washington, called L. Patrick Gray III of the FBI on the morning of the 19th and said that he must be briefed on the Watergate burglary. The President, in Key Biscayne, Florida, was coming back to Washington on the evening of the 19th. It was clear that everybody was to meet on the 20th.

John Doar lived in a basement apartment of an old

brownstone house a block down from the hotel. The apartment had a kitchenette, a bedroom with no door, a living room with a pull-out couch for sleeping. Doar and his daughter stayed in the apartment. Doar left the front door open all night in case Bob Owen finally caved in and came down for a nap. The Capitol Hill section at night is a place of triple locks and guard dogs.

In the middle of the second night of working with Owen, Doar slipped down the block for a nap of his own. He was awakened by the sound of somebody padding around the living room. Doar looked up and saw enough in the darkness to tell that it was a prowler, not anybody he knew.

"Get the fuck out of here," Doar said.

The prowler walked out and Doar went back to sleep.

At 6:30 p.m. on his third day, Bob Owen stopped work and walked down to Doar's apartment. He slept for three hours. He went back and began dictating notes for the summary. As Owen dictated, something was bothering him. He stopped, had a cup of coffee, lit a cigarette, and thought. He wanted to go back to the cards again. File drawers banged open and fingers went through the files, pulling out the index cards. Owen spread them out again and began looking.

"Now this is awfully peculiar," he said. He began to arrange them. His arrangement showed that on the morning of June 20, 1972, Richard Nixon had breakfast at 8:40. At nine o'clock he was in his Oval Office. From 9:01 until 9:04, Alexander Butterfield came in. Then from 9:04 until 10:20, the President sat alone in his office. He neither received nor placed any phone calls. Upstairs, in the office directly overhead, H. R. Haldeman met with John Ehrlichman and John Mitchell at 9 a.m. John Dean and Richard Kleindienst joined the meeting. The meeting lasted for an hour. The burglary had taken place early on the morning of June 17. This was the President's first day back in the White House since the burglary. It was the first day his staff had assembled and held a meeting since the burglary. Nixon knew they were meeting about the burglary. Yet from 9:04 a.m. until 10:20 a.m., the cards in front of Bob Owen showed, Nixon never once picked up the phone to ask his people upstairs one question about a burglary that was all over the front pages of the newspapers. And this was a President who interfered in even the most minor of matters—picking the color of a rug for an assistant's office.

It was clear what Nixon was doing in his office on the morning of June 20. He had ordered his people to fix the Watergate mess—can it, kill it, bury it—and he was taking the position that he did not want to know anything about it. This is the pattern and behavior of any boss-thief: you go do it, but don't tell me about it.

Owen called Doar in to look at the cards. Others crowded into the room. The cards showed it was not until 10:20 that Nixon spoke to anybody. And then he spoke to Ehrlichman. Both Nixon and Ehrlichman were claiming that they never had spoken about the Watergate. Ehrlichman was just coming out of the big meeting about the mess and he and Nixon, who dealt in colors of rugs, never mentioned the biggest story in the country. Then from 11:26 until 12:46, in his office in the Executive Office Building, Nixon spoke with H. R. Haldeman. There was a tape of that meeting. Eighteen and a half minutes of the tape had been erased. Nixon had sent his attorneys into court with all sorts of theories about how the tape was erased. The good General Alexander Haig said he thought it was the work of the Devil. Secretary Rose Mary Woods said she might have done it with her foot while leaning across the desk to answer a phone. She posed for a picture to justify this theory. In the picture she appeared to be sliding into third base. Meanwhile, anybody with any sense in the White House knew who had erased the tape. Nixon had erased the tape. "He was the only one could have done that," Dean Burch says today.

So now as Doar and Owen and the others stood in the organized litter of the library, with its barred, wired windows, with its red eyes and cigarettes and coffee, they knew they had it put together.

For much earlier, back on May 14, John Doar had presented to the Judiciary Committee the first piece of his information about Richard Nixon's activities on the first few days immediately following the Watergate break-in. It turned up in Book II of Doar's series of presentations to the committee. The title of Book II was, "Statement of Information; Events Following the Watergate Break-In. June 17, 1972–February 9, 1973." He read the book aloud with the same verve used in writing the titles. Doar read to the Committee behind locked doors and under strange, delicate, intricate rules. He was counsel for the entire Committee and therefore an impartial voice, not an advocate. He was careful to have no opinion in word or tone. Doar also was an employee of the Committee, not an elected Congressman. The distinction has no subtleties. Congressmen often view the people working around them as primarily chauffeurs and errand boys. No matter how unobtrusive Doar became, how silently diligent, some Committee members still glared at him as if he had stepped across the line drawn by the ballot box. Rodino is specifically excluded here. But the attitude on the part of some of the others would produce sharp trouble later on.

On May 14, during the afternoon, Doar read to the Committee with his dead voice and when he came to page 36, his voice had even less in it.

"On June 23, 1972, H. R. Haldeman met with the President and informed the President of the communication John Dean had received from Acting FBI Director Gray. The President directed Haldeman to meet with CIA Director Richard Helms, Deputy CIA Director Vernon Walters and John Ehrlichman. . . . The President directed Haldeman to discuss White House concern regarding possible disclosure of covert CIA operations and operations of the White House Special Investigations Unit [the 'Plumbers'], not related to Watergate, that had been undertaken previously by some of the Watergate principals. The President directed Haldeman to ask Walters to meet with Gray to express these concerns and to coordinate with the FBI, so that the FBI's investigation would not be expanded into unrelated matters that could lead to disclosure of the earlier activities of the Watergate principals."

In footnotes, Doar had listed his sources and on which page of their thick notebooks Congressmen could locate them:

31.1 *H. R. Haldeman testimony, Subcommittee of the Senate Appropriations Committee, Hearings on Purported Attempt to Involve the Central Intelligence Agency in the Watergate and Ellsberg incidents, Executive Session, May 31, 1973, 353-54*   PAGE 356

31.2 *President Nixon statement, May 23, 1973, Presidential documents, 693,696*   PAGE 358

31.3 *H. R. Haldeman testimony, 8 SSC 3040-41*   PAGE 360

31.4 *H. R. Haldeman testimony, 7 SSC 2884*   PAGE 362

James St. Clair, Nixon's lawyer, sat in the room while the reading went on. There was no way to miss what it was about: Doar was showing that an obstruction of justice occurred on June 23, 1972, and that it was started by Richard Nixon. That on this date, in 1972, he knew everything about the Watergate break-in. St. Clair sat in his chair. His defense for Nixon was based on the President never learning anything until March 21, 1973. St. Clair gave no indication that he realized the danger in Doar's approach. Nor did he subsequently realign his defenses. The man was spread too thin to do much about it anyway, and he appeared to like the television lights too much to have any confrontations with his client that might lead to a new lawyer.

At another point in the reading, Doar droned out this: "At approximately one-thirty p.m. on June 23, 1972, pursuant to the President's prior directions, H. R. Haldeman, John Ehrlichman, CIA Director Helms, and Deputy CIA Director Walters sat in Ehrlichman's office. . . . Haldeman stated that it was the President's wish that Walters call on Gray and suggest to him that it was not advantageous to push the inquiry, especially into Mexico. According to Ehrlichman, the Mexican money or the Florida bank account was discussed as a specific example of the kind of thing the President was evidently concerned about."

As he read the Ehrlichman material, Doar could almost hear a cheer going up from the people back in his library. It was a burial job. The footnote on the page directed Committee members to Ehrlichman's testimony before the Ervin committee. At that time, all newsmen reported that Ehrlichman had put on a great show, sneering and fighting right down the line. But Ehrlichman had a habit of sometimes forgetting what he was talking about and when somebody brought up the checks from Mexico, Ehrlichman said, of course, the Mexican money. Yes, that's exactly what the President was concerned about. Nobody noticed what he was saying, and the day passed. But when they sat in John Doar's library and began chopping up Ehrlichman's Ervin testimony, they thought his statement about the checks was absolutely marvelous. With other material they could prove that on

June 20, 1972, Maurice Stans had conducted meetings about covering up the Mexican checks. Ehrlichman, the perfect stonewall, had added greatly to the story.

When he was finished reading, Doar asked the Committee to subpoena the White House tape of June 23, 1972, which, his cards showed, featured Nixon and Haldeman in another discussion. This was the tape which Evan Davis, in his wheelchair, had wanted. There was a drawerful of blank subpoenas in Doar's office, presigned by Pat Jennings, Clerk of the House. One of the blanks was typed up, carbons everywhere, and signed by Peter Rodino. Ben Marshall, a Committee employee, carried it over to the White House.

* * *

At this time, Nixon still was not listening to the tapes himself. Only one man had heard all the tapes, Haldeman. When Nixon checked with Haldeman, in California, on this latest subpoena of a tape, for June 23, a tingle of fear had to run along the telephone lines. Somebody over in the Judiciary was onto the game.

Doar was convinced that the White House never would give the tapes to his group. But at the same time he was beginning to become convinced that he was going to be able to build a case without any of the tapes at all. He was confident that he was going to prove it all with paper, prove that the President knew of Watergate and initiated a cover-up on June 23, 1972. If the Special Prosecutor's office went through the courts and was given the tape, fine. The House Judiciary Committee neither recognized any court's authority nor had the time to wait.

So the paper rustled, and Richard Nixon, never hearing it, kept up his public lie. In his office one day he jumped out of his chair and began pacing up and down, throwing his arms out, and saying to Leonard

Garment, one of his counsels, "I go to China, go to Russia, we're trying to stop war in the Middle East. And to get tripped up by this . . . by this piece of shit!"

And now there was more. As Doar and Owen looked at their cards, they saw a clear picture of why and how Nixon operated from the very start, the first full day of the cover-up of the Watergate break-in. There had been a crime committed by people working for the President and the President says he did not inquire about it. He met with Ehrlichman. He did not ask. He met with Haldeman. He did not ask. Nixon maintained that it was not until nine months later, on March 21, 1973, that he first learned the facts of the Watergate break-in, learned them from John Dean.

As Doar and Owen looked at the cards, small sarcastic voices seemed to be everywhere:

Come on!

They knew the same voices would run through the minds of most of the Committee members as they began to hear the last of the evidence.

It was morning now. Owen walked down the street to Doar's apartment and took a shower. He came back to the library and started dictating notes. On his fourth straight day of work, sitting amidst a sea of paper, he was dictating more dangerous words onto paper, whose edges twinkled as the light hit its honed edges. This time Richard Nixon did not feel it as his head was being cut off.

* * *

On July 20th, 1974, on the day that John Doar really showed his teeth in the Judiciary Committee room, he came at them with this:

"On that morning of June 20th [1972], Mr. Haldeman, and you have got this all in your books, the logs, and everywhere, Mr. Haldeman meets with Ehrlichman and Mitchell at nine o'clock in the morning. Dean and Kleindienst joined that meeting, and they meet from nine to ten o'clock. This is the first day that the President has come back faced with a possibility of certainly a very serious scandal within his Administration.

"What does the President do while his people, his key advisers are discussing this matter? The President is alone in his office, except for a three-minute talk with Mr. Butterfield during that morning until John Ehrlichman comes in and talks to him about ten-twenty. He does not participate, does not inquire, does not question, does not search out for facts from John Mitchell or Richard Kleindienst, his Attorney General, or Mr. Ehrlichman, who has been assigned to the case the day before to make an investigation, or two days before, or from John Dean, who had been called back to get into it. . . ."

James Mann read. Tom Railsback read. Hamilton Fish, Jr., read. Caldwell Butler read. Ray Thornton read. Walter Flowers read. Harold Froehlich read.

10

"*God save the United States of America.*"

* * *

On July 24th, at 11 a.m., two college students from Cambridge, Charles Sheppard and Fred Hyatt, leaned forward in their seats inside the Supreme Court, eyes fixed on the front of the room, four white pillars with red velvet behind the pillars, sculpturing of Romans above a clock. The Supreme Court in a minute or so was to issue its decision on whether President Nixon had to release a batch of sixty-four tapes subpoenaed by Special Prosecutor Leon Jaworski. One of the tapes was for the day of June 23, 1972. John Doar was going it without the June 23 tape, the one Evan Davis, in the wheelchair, had wanted to get at the day he began his job. But Jaworski's office was not going without the tapes. The case had gone to the Supreme Court and now these two college students, people whom Nixon hated when he was on the top,

165

were waiting for the decision. At 11:03, a voice called out, "The Honorable Chief Justice Burger and the Associate Justices of the Supreme Court of the United States. Oyez, oyez, all having business before this honorable court draw near. God save the United States of America."

The minute William O. Douglas came out, the two college kids poked each other. You did not have to be a courtroom buff to see that Douglas was relaxed, a near-smile on his face. Of course the kids looked at Douglas first. For so long, in this country, Douglas was about all they had going for them. Burger ruffled papers in front of him. Docket number 731766, *United States* versus *Richard Nixon*; Docket number 731834, *Nixon* versus *United States*. Nixon's entire case was whether executive privilege allowed him to keep the tapes confidential. When Burger began reading, Douglas looked even better. The knockout was coming.

The courtroom was filled. Since dawn there had been long lines waiting outside on the marble steps. Gold grill-work separated the press, crowded onto the side of the huge old room, from the audience. This was an important day, a regal day. The lawyers and more scholarly writers tend to deify the Supreme Court. And at this time they looked at the Court as the place which would finally destroy Nixon. Which was fine but the Supreme Court not only reads the newspapers, it attends cocktail parties and eats dinner out in restaurants, and all members have phones and visitors at home. As they sat in their robed splendor, they had to know the way things stood across the street, in the Senate and House, and in the House Judiciary, as well as anybody. "The vote will be eight to zero," O'Neill told me the day before. I asked him how he knew. "Constitutional lawyers at Harvard told me," he said.

Now, as Warren Burger read his decision, he came to his first "however," and this is a word, this "how-

ever," which has killed more people than field artil-
lery. It is listed as a conjunction, but it should be
assigned a number, like .155.

"However, the special prosecutor . . . has authority
to represent the United States as a sovereign. . . ."
From the "however," Burger went into *Marbury* versus *Madison*. This is a decision which set the su-
premacy of the Court in legal matters—no man is
above the Court. Since Special Prosecutor Jaworski
was sitting there with all the Court orders in his
pocket, it was reasonable to assume that the re-
mainder of Mr. Burger's reading was to be as bad for
Mr. Nixon as it turned out to be.

Nixon had to turn over the sixty-four tapes, including the tape of June 23.

As Jaworski went down the steps of the Supreme
Court, with the young people crowding around him
and cheering, and the reporters guiding him to live
network-television cameras, it was one of those days
when people in the profession say proudly that the law
has prevailed. The jealous mistress had triumphed
again. Perhaps, or perhaps it had triumphed because
the people conducting the business of the law had an
essentially abstract matter on their hands, and it also
had about three hundred votes going for it across the
way in the House of Representatives. Historically, the
Supreme Court always functions beautifully at these
times. And nowhere in the decision was it stated that
if the Supreme Court did not come out unanimously
for Nixon to give up the tapes, if the Chief Justice, appointed by Nixon, did not read the decision himself,
then the Court, as an institution, would have been
irrelevant at a great moment in the nation's history
and damaged forever. For Nixon was going out of his
job, no matter how the Court voted. And the Chief
Justice himself would have been suspect and a personal laughingstock if he himself did not read the decision.

Supportive evidence for this theory can be found in

the activity of the Court on the very next day, July 25th. When, with virtually no publicity and with no strong sense of what Congress wanted, the Court made a ruling on an important human matter, the Detroit metropolitan school-busing case. In this case, the city of Detroit had asked to be allowed to bus, for integration purposes, blacks from the city of Detroit across the city line and into metropolitan suburbs. The Supreme Court voted against the busing plan. The Burgers, Blackmuns, Rehnquists—the white men appointed to the bench by a white crook—were in the majority. Dissenting was, of course, Douglas:

> *Desegregation is not and was never expected to be an easy task. Racial attitudes ingrained in our Nation's childhood and adolescence are not quickly thrown aside in its middle years. But just as the inconvenience of some cannot be allowed to stand in the way of the rights of others, so public opposition, no matter how strident, cannot be permitted to divert this Court from the enforcement of the constitutional principles at issue in this case. Today's holding, I fear, is more a reflection of a perceived public mood that we have gone far enough in enforcing the Constitution's guarantee of equal justice than it is the product of neutral principles of law. In the short run, it may seem to be the easier course to allow our great metropolitan areas to be divided up each into two cities—one white, the other black—but it is a course, I predict, our people will ultimately regret. I dissent.*

But on the previous morning, July 24th, with a decision involving tapes and principles, neither of which has blood running through the arteries, the Supreme Court could afford to be an anchor of civilization. The inscription on the outside of the building, running across its eight pillars, "Equal Justice Under Law," nearly seemed real on this day.

Across the street, across the square of dripping trees and damp grass, there sat on the steps of the Capitol the only demonstrators seen in Washington during the entire time of impeachment and resignation. The young, sadly disciplined followers of Sun Myung Moon stood in vigil in the muggy air, holding a sign announcing which member of the House each was praying for, to save his soul from certain damnation if he chose to vote against Nixon. One of the young people, who came from Alaska, did not know how to spell Moon's name. "I never had reason to spell it before," he said. He was living in one of Moon's religious dens in Tarrytown, New York.

Aside from these demonstrators, who had the effect of depressing all who saw them, there was nothing.

It was strange to be around when it happened, because it was an enormous thing and it had never happened before; but there still was so very little to see in Washington in the summer of 1974. White marble sitting in swamp heat. On this day, on the 24th, the news of the Supreme Court decision should have "rocked" the White House and the nation. It did no such thing. Oh, it wasted Nixon some more. The flesh turned pasty and the eyes hollowed and the flesh under the chin fell through the muscles. He was out at San Clemente when the news of the decision was announced. The story circulated that Nixon had attempted to walk into the ocean and drown himself. The great scene from *A Star Is Born*. James Mason going into the ocean while Judy Garland sings. The story was untrue. General Haig, however, apparently did get his hands on Nixon's tranquilizers. The essential Roman Catholic mind: die by the gun if you must, but an overdose of narcotics is sinful; that's for the weirdos.

But, otherwise, there was no turmoil, no racing through corridors, no people screaming out windows.

In the White House, people for the first time began
to glance out the windows to see that the avalanche
of paper had started to pound the ground away from
the building much as the ocean washes out the under-
pinnings of a beach house. It was only a matter of
time. By now it was coming from so many places—
the Court, from Jaworski, from Sirica, from Congress,
from the newspapers and television, over the phones,
in the mail—that it was just a matter of which method
did the job first. Yet nowhere in Washington were
there voices raised. The hallways and cafeterias of
the Capitol were crowded with tourists from America.
Cameras, bare, tan springy legs, cut-off jeans. Children running down a marble hallway ahead of par-
ents. Don't want to look at the statue, want to go
down and look out that window. The young ones,
boys and girls alike, all seemed to wear short-
sleeved replicas of football jerseys worn by professional teams. Through the swirl of cameras and jeans
and football jerseys, here was Hugh Scott walking to
meet Barry Goldwater.

At the House end of the building one day, O'Neill
came out of his office and a boy with American short
blond hair and wearing a replica of a Pittsburgh Steel-
ers jersey bumped into him. Gulliver plays football.
O'Neill went down the hall, picking his way through
the tourists, to attend a meeting at which John
Rhodes, the Republican leader in the House, gave it
one last try for Nixon. Rhodes said he wanted the impeachment resolution recommitted with instructions
that there should be a vote on censuring the President.

"I'm bitterly opposed to that," O'Neill said.

"But you wouldn't be opposed to us having a vote
on censure, would you?" Rhodes said.

"Yes, I would," O'Neill said.

On the night of the 24th, the House Judiciary Committee began its televised hearings. The moment Peter
Rodino began to speak directly into the camera, speak

solemnly, powerfully, there was nothing left. There were thirty-eight members of the Committee. There were not at this time thirty-eight people from any walk of life in the nation—take any thirty-eight executives earning over a half-million a year—who could have stayed abreast with this group, for accuracy, for style, for perception, for understanding of what it was that they were doing. Sometimes, each said the same things, but each was saying it in his own way, and you wanted to hear more of what each had to say, not less. When James Mann of South Carolina spoke, he caused the eyes to go out of focus, the mind to sway. He became distant, a figure from a painting, from a page in a history book, a figure who had lived a couple of hundred years ago.

* * *

On the way home to the Shoreham Hotel from a Chinese restaurant that first night, Roger Brooks, O'Neill's chauffeur, drove us slowly past the Capitol. The great white dome, washed in brilliant and yet subdued lighting, looked magnificent.

"No matter how many times I pass by it," O'Neill said, "I still get a feeling right in here." He punched his stomach with his fist. "It stands for stability. You see that dome up there, you know that nobody is going to let anything bad happen. You die before you let this country down."

On July 29th, O'Neill sat with the Republican Whip, Les Arends, in the back of a plane at National Airport, waiting for Vice President Ford to arrive. They were flying to a golf tournament in Massachusetts.

"Tip, you don't have all those votes," Arends said.

"Les, we're friends talking now. We're going to have three hundred votes in the House. Now we're talking as friends. And let me tell you something else. He's dead in the Senate. He doesn't have twenty-four votes in the Senate, I can tell you that right now."

"Where are you getting this from?" Arends said.

"Hey, I'm getting it from the floor. I'm out there every day. I get it from the members."

"Well, that isn't the figures we're getting," Arends said.

"Well, where are yours coming from?" O'Neill asked him.

"From the White House," Arends said.

"You've got to be kidding," O'Neill said.

When Ford came on the plane, Arends went to him and had him listen to O'Neill's figures. Ford had said he did not want to hear anything about being President. A politician, however, will listen to arithmetic. As Ford heard O'Neill's figures, his face changed.

O'Neill relaxed on the plane and decided to tell a story about Elliot Richardson. After all, Ford would need a Vice President and there was no harm in telling him about Elliot Richardson.

"When Richardson was the Attorney General of Massachusetts he went after a man eighteen months after the fella died, I never heard anything like it in my life," O'Neill said. "Bill Callahan. He was the Commissioner of the Massachusetts Turnpike Authority. When Bill died, his secretary, Helen Healy, emptied the contents of the wall safe in Callahan's office. So Richardson has her subpoenaed before the grand jury which was going after Callahan, who has been dead for eighteen months now. So they put Helen Healy on the stand and the prosecutor asks her, "Did you not empty the contents of the Commissioner's safe?' And Helen Healy says, 'Yes, I did.' And she is asked, 'What did the contents consist of?' And she says, 'Oh, I couldn't tell you that.' The prosecutor says, 'I direct you to answer.' They have to call a recess and Helen sees her lawyer out in the hallway and then she comes back into the grand jury room and the prosecutor says, 'Now, I ask you again. You emptied the contents of the Turnpike Commissioner Callahan's wall safe, did you not?" And she says, "Yes, I did.' And the prosecutor says, 'Now I ask you what did the contents of the safe consist of?' And Helen Healy said, 'Ten thousand Xerox copies of Elliot Richardson's 1939 drunken-driving record.' " (In Boston they never throw anything away—not even the drunken-driving record of an eighteen-year-old.)

O'Neill's roar rang out through the plane, along with Ford's.

"I'd never heard that one," Ford said.

"Now you have," O'Neill said proudly.

At the golf tournament, Ford and O'Neill walked down the fairway together, arms behind each other's back. Pictures were snapped. The picture ran everyplace. The Republican Vice President and the Democratic House Majority Leader. O'Neill mentioned the picture as being of great humor. As a professional politician, there was no reason for him to mention the unspoken agreements that had caused the picture to be taken. Proper practice is to turn to the humor of the act. The White House, however, regarded the picture as exactly what it was: a final eviction notice.

* * *

On Friday, August 2nd, in the White House staff dining room, a small, noisy room in the basement, Leonard Garment, J. Fred Buzhardt, Jr., William Timmons, and Dean Burch had lunch. There was a discussion of what Nixon had to do. There were only two options. Everybody had looked out the windows and saw that by now the flood of paper had the building up on pilings, with the paper eating through the creosote on the pilings and into the wood. One option was for Nixon to see it through to a certain loss. The other was for him to resign. Leonard Garment was in favor of resignation. Buzhardt said nothing to him.

173

After lunch, on the way back to their offices in the Executive Office Building across the alley from the White House, Buzhardt said to Garment, "He's going to have to resign. Some of this new stuff on the tapes we have to turn over to Jaworski is very bad."

Over the weekend, Nixon went to Camp David with Alexander Haig and Raymond Price and Pat Buchanan. It was obvious the last two were there to write something. On Sunday, Dean Burch received a phone call at his home from Haig.

"We've got problems with these new tapes Jaworski is to receive," Haig said. "But it's nothing we can't deal with."

Burch said that was fine. Then at 8:30 on Monday morning, August 5, 1974, he went to his office in the White House. Timmons and Ken Clawson, the deputy communications director, were to be briefed on the weekend by Pat Buchanan.

"Now about this tape," Buchanan said. He went over what was on the tape of June 23, 1972. As Buchanan finished, Burch was getting up and reaching for something.

"All I can conclude," Buchanan said, "is that the Old Man has been shitting us."

Burch now had in hand what he had been reaching for. A bottle of bourbon.

"Let's have a drink," Burch said.

Later that day, later on Monday, August 5, 1974, at a few minutes after three o'clock, there arrived on the floor of the House of Representatives a page girl in white blouse and blue slacks, carrying a sheaf of long paper. The floor was less than a quarter occupied at the time, but among those present was O'Neill. O'Neill's heavy freckled hand reached out to take a copy from the page; two sheets stapled together, letter-spaced typing. Tip O'Neill held the paper away from him and began reading it aloud, a small group standing around his seat and listening to his deep North Cambridge street tones.

"For immediate release. Office of the White House Press Secretary. The White House. Statement by the President: I have today instructed my attorneys to make available to the House Judiciary Committee, and I am making public, the transcripts of three conversations with H. R. Haldeman on June 23, 1972. I have also turned over the tapes of these conversations to Judge Sirica as part of the process of my compliance with the Supreme Court ruling.

"On April 29, in announcing my decision to make public the original set of White House transcripts, I stated that 'as far as what the President personally knew and did with regard to Watergate and the cover-up is concerned, these materials, together with those already made available—will tell it all.' Shortly after that . . ."

O'Neill read on. He kept looking for the word "resign" or a synonym thereof. For many weeks now he had assumed that somebody in the White House would break through the numbness and inform Nixon that he was through. But as he read, the words O'Neill expected to see did not jump at him from the page, the way things of importance are supposed to do. The statement wandered through sentences which became paragraphs of words that were a half-notch off true meaning, and all delayed what had to be said. The preamble to Confession can only make you look worse, which is why Catholics use only one sentence— "Bless me Father for I have sinned, it has been six months since my last Confession . . ." before going right into the account of sin. Nixon attempting to make his first confession straggled about with these dreadful amateurisms: ". . . although I recognized these presented potential problems . . . I did realize the implications. . . ." Sitting in the House O'Neill droned on, turned the page, and now, finally, here it was, on the top of the second sheet:

"The June 23 tapes clearly show, however, that at the time I gave these instructions [to the CIA and

FBI] I also discussed the political aspects of the situation, and I was aware of the advantages this course of action would have with respect to limiting the possible public exposure of involvement by persons connected with the Re-Election Committee."

It was over. Richard Nixon's story, his front, his alibi, had lasted for 780 days. He had damn-near proved Lincoln wrong.

When O'Neill finished his dramatic reading, he walked off the floor, took the elevator the one flight down, and ambled into his suite of offices. He held the paper out for anybody who wanted it.

"Well, here it is. Confession is good for the soul, but it doesn't save the body."

He then got down to work that was of high importance to him at a time such as this. He had to call his wife, Milly Miller O'Neill, at Harwichport, on Cape Cod, and tell her to get her clothes together because she was going to see a new President sworn in. When his wife asked him when, O'Neill told her that Nixon probably would be out within forty-eight hours. Milly Miller O'Neill said he could give her a call when the President was finished officially; she was staying at the Cape until then. Under the best of circumstances, she is not too strong on great ceremonies; when O'Neill's own John F. Kennedy was inaugurated, Milly Miller O'Neill said it was too cold for her to sit on a wooden chair on cement steps, and she stayed in a hotel a block away from the Capitol and watched it on television. It would take much to move her to see Nixon under any circumstance. Finally, on Thursday morning, August 8, 1974, daughter Rosemary O'Neill, who works in Washington, stopped at her father's office and he gave her the assignment of getting her mother down to Washington immediately.

"Mother," she said on the phone, "Dad says you better get dressed and come down here. He's got a room for you at the Jefferson."

"A suite," somebody called out.

"A nice suite," Rosemary said.

Rosemary hung up. "Dad, she says she has to drive to Cambridge to get a dress. She doesn't have any dresses with her at the Cape. So she won't be able to drive all the way home and still get a plane tonight. She'll be on the first plane in the morning."

At 2:44 on that Thursday afternoon, Eleanor Kelley, O'Neill's secretary, buzzed him. "The Vice President," she said.

O'Neill was in a long, narrow back office that he uses for eating diet lunches. He punched a button on a green telephone bank. His face broke into a laugh. For months, O'Neill had been saying to Ford on the phone, "Say, Jerry, I heard every time it rains, you call up the White House and tell them to close the windows." This time Ford opened up the conversation by discussing the golf picture of the two that was in the issue of *Newsweek* magazine. In mentioning the picture, Ford talked to O'Neill about it being a funny picture; they appeared to be picking each other's pockets. "Well, we sure had a helluva time," Ford said. He then got down to what he was calling about: Richard Nixon was submitting a letter of resignation to Henry Kissinger at 10:00 a.m. on the next morning, August 9th. The resignation would be effective at noon. Ford then would be sworn in at noon, and he asked that O'Neill be present.

"Are wives invited, Jerry?" O'Neill said. "The reason I'm asking is that I've already told Milly to pack herself up and get down here."

"Wives were not invited, but they are now," Ford said.

"Now Jerry, I've got a statement prepared and I'll read it for you." He picked up a typed release.

"While we are close personal friends and I have great respect for his honesty, integrity, and ability, our political philosophies are diametrically opposed. I wish him every success in bringing our politically torn country together. He can expect cooperation from Congress and I trust he will cooperate with Congress and most of America in the days ahead."

"That's fine, Tip. And I want to say I'll be relying on you for your advice and assistance."

"I can tell you one thing, Jerry, don't think of a Democrat for Vice President. This country doesn't work that way."

"Thanks for the advice."

"Christ, Jerry, isn't this a wonderful country? Here we can talk like this and you and I can be friends and eighteen months from now I'll be going around the country kicking your balls in."

That Thursday night, Nixon went on television to announce his resignation. He refused to make anything more than a vague acknowledgment that something wrong had occurred. First, he did not want to admit anything to anybody. And second, he did not at this time have a pardon deal worked out, therefore anything he said about himself might have returned to bother him at a later date. Later that night, Nixon called a friend of mine, who had worked for him in the White House, and said good-by.

"He talked about going to jail," my friend tells. "He was saying to me, 'Well, if they want to go all the way with me, I guess it won't be so bad. You can do a lot of political writing in jail. Lots of political books were written in jail. Just give me a table and a pad and pencils and let me go to work. No telephones to bother me. Yes, a lot of heads of state have gone to jail. Gandhi went to prison, you know.' "

It is very common for defendants to spread the belief that prison will kill them. People in Washington, who are unused to everyday life, made Nixon's health the basis for his pardon.

* * *

On the following Monday, August 12, 1974, here I was at a few minutes before nine o'clock at night, sitting in a chair on the floor of the House of Representatives. Brown leather, wine-red carpeting with flower patterns, polished brass spittoons, and half-light which suddenly turned into hot white light as the banks of television lights began burning down on us. In the seats to my right were the Kennedys and McGoverns and Liz Holtzmans and Herman Badillos. In the seats directly in front of me were these muscular African diplomats in white dashikis and skullcaps talking high Oxford English; the man in front of me, with shoulders like two brick stoops, sounding like Alistair Cooke, should thank God nightly that he was born in the jungles of Africa. If he was born in Washington, he would speak in unintelligible mumbles from getting slugged around as an underpaid offensive guard with the Redskins.

The television lights, banks of thousand-watt bulbs clamped to the ceiling of the old chamber, were beginning to outrun the air conditioning, first movements of discomfort showing in the crowd lining the walls, this ending immediately upon the sight of William (Fishbait) Miller, the House doorkeeper, stomping down the aisle, calling out in best Southern Baptist voice, "Mister Speaker, the President of the United States." When the doors swung open and everybody in the chamber saw that it was not Richard Nixon walking in, the cheers that went up around me on the floor were merely perfunctory when matched with the feeling of relief, a feeling so intense that it could be felt, almost heard, as it rose from their chests and shoulders to leave them free of Nixon and all the name meant to their careers and their country. Oh, they liked Jerry Ford very much. He had been one of them; his success might mean their success. But for anybody who was standing up with the crowd, watching, listening, feeling, it was obvious that these men, who are in politics for a living, would have cheered for anybody.

Ford stood at the rostrum, stood in the lights and

the noise, folded his hands behind his back, just folded them lightly, the thumbs hooked. I watched his hands very closely. They were not clenched in tension. When Ford spoke, he did so effortlessly, he needed no water, there was no throat-clearing, no sudden hand or body motions to break the pressure. The world watched, but Ford seemed to be talking to a small gathering of friends. For this one night anyway, Jim Hartz had just become President.

* * *

The next day, the first thing O'Neill and Leo Diehl did was to make reservations on the 6:40 p.m. Delta Airlines to Boston. They would have something to eat at Jimmy's Harborside and then drive down to the Cape for a few days. They discussed the reservations and plans with the same intensity which had gone into the talk of impeachment throughout the preceding weeks.

This was the problem for the day, getting to the 6:40 Delta to Boston, to Jimmy's Harborside, and then on to the Cape and George McCue's piano. Yesterday, the country shook. That was yesterday.

In mid-afternoon, new President Ford's secretary called O'Neill's office. He was having his first state dinner on Friday night, honoring the Shah of Iran. The new President Ford was inviting Congressman and Mrs. O'Neill to the dinner.

"I'll have to see," O'Neill said.

He called Milly Miller O'Neill at Harwichport, Cape Cod. He told her that there was this invitation to the new President's first state dinner, honoring the Shah of Iran, and did she feel like coming down to Washington for it?

"You've got to be kidding," Milly Miller O'Neill said. "A state dinner? I'm at the Cape and I'm staying. Which Delta are you making tonight?"

"We're on the six-forty."

"Well, don't miss it," she said.

The invitation from the new President was respectfully declined.

The Capitol building became empty early that day. At six-fifteen, O'Neill called to Eleanor Kelley, his secretary, "Is Roger ready to go?"

"He's outside already," she said.

"Well, we're off."

Leo Diehl already was out in the hallway. O'Neill stuck a Daniel Webster cigar into his mouth, said goodnight to Eleanor Kelley, and left.

The long marble hallway was silent and deserted and softly lit for the evening. Leo Diehl was halfway down it, body swinging in the air between his crutches. O'Neill walked slowly. He began to hum. Softly first. He took a breath and hummed louder. Now he took the cigar out of his mouth and started to sing.

> *Some of them write to the old folks at home,*
> *That's their old ace in the hole. . . .*

Up the hallway, Leo Diehl picked it up and now the two sang together as they went down the long marble hallway of the empty Capitol, leaving after the summer of 1974 and singing:

> *The others have girls on the old tenderloin,*
> *That's their old ace in the hole. . . .*